M000286989

Martin Buber's Dialogue

Martin Buber's Dialogue

—— Discovering Who We Really Are ——

Kenneth Paul Kramer

FOREWORD BY
Robert C. Morgan

CASCADE *Books* · Eugene, Oregon

MARTIN BUBER'S DIALOGUE
Discovering Who We Really Are

Copyright © 2019 Kenneth Paul Kramer. All rights reserved. Except for brief quotations in critical publications or reviews, no part of this book may be reproduced in any manner without prior written permission from the publisher. Write: Permissions, Wipf and Stock Publishers, 199 W. 8th Ave., Suite 3, Eugene, OR 97401.

Cascade Books
An Imprint of Wipf and Stock Publishers
199 W. 8th Ave., Suite 3
Eugene, OR 97401

www.wipfandstock.com

PAPERBACK ISBN: 978-1-5326-6575-2
HARDCOVER ISBN: 978-1-5326-6576-9
EBOOK ISBN: 978-1-5326-6577-6

Cataloguing-in-Publication data:

Names: Kramer, Kenneth, 1941–, author. | Morgan, Robert C., foreword.

Title: Martin Buber's dialogue : discovering who we really are / by Kenneth Paul Kramer ; foreword by Robert C. Morgan.

Description: Eugene, OR: Cascade Books, 2019. | Includes bibliographical references and index.

Identifiers: ISBN 978-1-5326-6575-2 (paperback). | ISBN 978-1-5326-6576-9 (hardcover). | ISBN 978-1-5326-6577-6 (ebook).

Subjects: LCSH: Buber, Martin, 1878–1965. | Dialogue—Interdisciplinary aspects. | Dialogue analysis.

Classification: P95.455 K73 2019 (print). | P95.455 (ebook).

Manufactured in the U.S.A.   09/27/19

To Harold Kasimow

George Drake Professor of Religious Studies
Emeritus, Grinnell College

Colleague, Friend, and Dialogical Partner

I must say it once again. I have no teaching. I only point to something . . . I point to something in reality that had not or had too little been seen. I take him who listens to me by the hand and lead him to the window. I open the window and point to what is outside. I have no teaching, but I carry on a conversation.

—MARTIN BUBER

Contents

Foreword

I HAVE AN IMAGE of Kenneth Kramer playing basketball at the Andover Newton Theological Seminary in the autumn of 1964. He had just retrieved a rebound. A brief pause followed, and then a sudden move to the right. Within a split second he jumped up and dropped the ball through the hoop. I recall Ken's athletic finesse as being relatively impeccable. His timing was superb. I wanted to get to know him, to understand his thinking, which is probably the reason I was invited more than fifty years later to introduce his recent book, *Martin Buber's Dialogue: Discovering Who We Really Are.*

One of my first conversations with Ken was in his corner dormitory room. We focused on an arbitrary group of European theologians that students referred to as the four B's. They included Dietrich Bonhoeffer, Karl Barth, Rudolf Bultmann, and finally Martin Buber—all great scholars who had revolutionized theology by giving it a more secular, existential approach. I recall my liberal emotional tendencies were difficult for Ken, especially when I portrayed myself as an earnest radical bent on liberating myself from the stagnant Protestant rhetoric on which I had been raised. I soon discovered his background was coming from a very different place, which would require further extended dialogues to clarify and finally to come to an understanding of one another.

As the years drifted by, these differences seemed to fall in place. Things began changing for both of us. I remember the first occasion I had to read one of his exegeses on Buber, my reception was enormously positive. He seemed intent on delivering a masterfully crafted text. Without ignoring the subtle complexity of what his "teacher's teacher" cites as a "genuine dialogue," or forgetting his early years tracking Zen Buddhism, Hinduism, and eventually Benedictine Catholicism, it made perfect sense that Buber should have a strong impact on Ken's thinking as he was in the process of forging a new scholarly direction. I have frequently considered him as someone living the reality of the dialogue even before he came to terms with its in-depth spiritual ramifications.

I base this realization on the author's remarkable sense of ease in knowing how to conduct his relationships with others as indicated in the various chapters of *Martin Buber's Dialogue*. It might also be attributed to the author's immense capacity to stay alert to what is happening around him just as he did on the basketball court many years ago. Could it be that Buber's writings gave his acolyte something he already knew about himself, *within* himself, only on a more conscious level? This would be difficult to ascertain and impossible to speculate. What we do know is that all of this would excel profoundly through the diligent encouragement of his larger-than-life mentor and colleague at Temple University, Professor Maurice Friedman.

At this juncture, I would like to make a few remarks about why I believe this is an important book. It is the most recent installment in a series of deeply penetrating texts on Martin Buber by Professor Kenneth Kramer. The current publication of *Martin Buber's Dialogue: Discovering Who We Really Are* suggests that the author has not as yet exhausted the possibilities by which to reveal fresh insights and radically innovative ideas on how to apply the words of one of the leading thinkers of the twentieth century to the way we live in the twenty-first. There is no doubt that the presence of Buber's dialogue continues to function ahead of its time, which gives it a necessary role in today's fast-paced environment despite its intermittent status as being infamously controversial.

Here I would like to offer a quote by the author from Chapter 4, titled "Responding," because I believe it represents clearly and without hesitation the fundamental reason why this book exists:

> According to Buber, everyone is dialogically constructed (both personally and socially) and dialogically directed (both instinctively and verbally). Further, the dialogical partner affirms our reciprocal and reciprocating responsibility in life. My stand, my place in the world is not just a function of willpower, is not just an attitude of mind. It also embodies an already-existing dimension, the influence of relational grace that joins with my willpower to affect my presence in the world. When I wholeheartedly and unreservedly respond to the other whom I encounter during the flow of events in my life, without holding back, again and again, I am able to become myself.[1]

1. See below, 99.

This passage moves me. I admire its ability to passionately objectify a potential subjective moment within a method of thought and behavior that allows me to understand the inextricable connection between myself and the other. Given Buber's emphasis on methodology, a major portion of *Martin Buber's Dialogue* is devoted to Professor Kramer's analysis of the four stages involved in Buber's dialogical philosophy. The four stages (in this order) are *turning, addressing, listening,* and *responding*. While Kramer has elected to deal with each of these separately, one cannot ignore the chance probability of how these gestural and verbal states of Being might concur both physically and emotionally within the same moment. For example, one may be *turning* toward the other at the same moment one is *listening*, thus creating a kind of spatial vignette in contrast to a normative sequence in time. In this case I would offer the possibility that there is a performative function inextricably bound to the dialogues (as I understand the author has shown in introducing comments by the actor Alan Alda).

While Professor Kramer is careful to make these tropes clear through examples of dialogues he has experienced in one form or another, the details may distract from the focus of our attention. From Buber's position, these distractions should not dissuade the participants from continuing their dialogue, but should be accepted as integral to the experience *whenever possible*. Although not mentioned in the book, I would argue in favor of the avant-garde composer John Cage's concept of "chance operations"— meaning that when indeterminate noise intervenes with predetermined or scored sound (music), it should become part of the performance, rather than summarily rejected as an exterior interruption.

The social and psychological dimensions of analysis employed in *Martin Buber's Dialogue* are pervasive to the extent that one may sense upon occasion a meandering use of repetition. While I hesitate to suggest this as a criticism, given the prescribed intention that Professor Kramer has so intelligently put forth in his superbly articulated "Introduction," it does suggest that something is missing. In other words, what is being left out of the analysis that might suggest a further direction in which Buber's dialogue might achieve a more pronounced relevance to where our global society is moving today? I would put it in the following way:

Since the predictable advances in the field of cybernetics and advanced information technologies, including recent applications of Artificial Intelligence, have more or less come true, where does this take Buber's dialogue? Is it still possible to introduce the enlightened concept "that 'genuine dialogue' is our human birthright" to a generation presumptuously addicted to incessant "texting" and proto-robotic behavior? My use of the term "generation" is perhaps less about age than the tendency for people to exist (rather than live) in a hypermediated environment primarily wired against intellect. Again, what are the chances they will find their way into a genuine dialogue where the other becomes the significant means to discovering who they really are?

There are other aspects to this argument that need to be taken into account as well. In addition to the psychological and social limitations that may or may not be present, there is the gradual loss of tactile sensation in our society. Here I refer to absence of touch or even the loss of memory in relation to touch. This would apply most importantly to touch in terms of a physical sensation, but also there is the emotional touch of how we feel in relation to experiencing a genuine dialogue, the resonance of the spoken word felt in conjunction with a human voice and a living human presence. One may also include touch in relation to objects, for example, as in holding an heirloom in one's hands that has been in the family for several generations or the sensation of holding freshly cut vegetables from the garden in our hands in contrast to purchasing processed food in synthetic packages.

To understand another person on the level that Martin Buber proposes implies more than words. It is words in relation to memory, which would include people, places, sounds, smells, tastes, nature, or objects that hold special significance. In many encounters, words lose their significance without a sense of touch, without the memory of how we feel in relation to the tactile environment that surrounds us. The impulse to touch still needs to be present, permissible, and available to our senses. This would seem to be an indispensable part of the genuine dialogue.

Despite these concerns, I believe Kenneth Kramer's book is one of the most significant contributions to dialogical literature currently available. For a creative scholar, such as Kramer, to remind us how to regenerate the art of conversation in an environment of facts and figures is an important and necessary gift. It offers a feasible alternative to the dialogical vacuum our society has become. The timing is perfect for the words of Martin Buber to reappear and to resonate, and for Kenneth Kramer to show us the ways in which this might happen.

Robert C. Morgan, PhD
Professor Emeritus, Art History
Rochester Institute of Technology

Preface

"Wait," I exclaimed, "that's not all!" I was discussing this book with an Indian student named Harp in the University of California, Santa Cruz pool locker room. We were each finishing dressing after showering, continuing our conversation that had begun in the shower. Standing at the end of a row of lockers, looking directly at me sitting at the other end, he had just asked, "What's 'dialogue' mean?"

"Ah," I had answered while simultaneously moving my left-hand back and forth between us. "This. What we are doing right now—sharing meaningful words between persons who are attentive to each other!"

"Oh," he said. His smile broadened, his eyes were singing.

"But . . . there's more," I said.

He was still drinking in his awareness that dialogue meant exactly what we were doing. "Then," I continued, "it turns out that when we travel on this dialogical path, the process allows us to discover our human authenticity."

Suddenly, he grew serious. "I want to read *that* book," he said.

It was as if he recognized that this book spoke to a deep question haunting him and that the book might make finding himself possible.

"I want to read *that* book," he reiterated before running off to his next class. *Martin Buber's Dialogue: Discovering Who We Really Are* is that book.

A new interaction takes place: a new beginning opens up. It is neither predetermined nor guaranteed to occur. But when real dialogue happens, time and space open out. Suddenly, it seems as if the entire universe is waiting for this interaction. Rather than being attentive and responsive, authentic dialogue occurs before its partners are aware of doing anything special.

The Problem

Why is this book exceptionally valuable?

First of all, *Martin Buber's Dialogue* is for beginners in a double sense. It is written for non-specialists, for those who have not studied, or thought about, or practiced dialogue.

In a sense, of course, we are all beginners in that we are always learning new things. Learning how to practice living dialogue is a bit like learning a new language where unfamiliar terms are explained with words we understand. And like learning a new language, we need to practice, and practice, and practice.

Yet, unlike learning a new language, here we need to reorient ourselves, or to put it simply, re-identify ourselves from *individuals* (who by definition remain separate and distinct from other individuals) to *persons* (who willingly enter two-sided events and conversations with others). An individual stands at the center of his or her own experience; a person seeks and is seized by opportunities to become inter-relational, to become dialogical with others. The person who takes a stand in and for relationship becomes authentic and unified.

We're living in fractious times. Life is not easy with its relentless reasons for becoming "frightened," "sorry," "confused," "saddened," and "deeply depressed." Yet by far, for me, the single reason, the reason beneath reasons to which difficult times can be attributed is what Alan Alda writes in *If I Understood You, Would I Have This Look On My Face?* Alda states that the underlying problem plaguing today's society is that—get this!— "pretty much everybody misunderstands everybody else," and "people are dying because we can't communicate in ways that allow us to understand one another."[2] Drink that in. We seem to prefer being at war with others than trying to understand each other.

Reflecting on a decade-long journey to discover new ways of helping people to more effectively communicate, Alda writes:

> In the dance of communication, we move together with another person gracefully, pleasurably, sharing the pure animal joy of community.
>
> Not being able to communicate is the Siberia of everyday life—a place that, crazily, we often send *ourselves* to.

---

2. Alda, *If I Understood You*, xiii.

> But the solution, in my view, isn't a formula, a list of tips, or a
> chart that shows where to put your feet. Instead, it's a transforming
> yourself-like going to the gym-only a whole lot more fun.
> Practicing contact with other people feels good.[3]

Not surprisingly, Alda's book stems from improvisational acting, from standing on the stage communicating face-to-face with other actors. Of course. What a great opportunity. I agree, at least with the first part of his answer: his disinterest in formulaic lists; his interest in "transforming yourself" and "practicing contact." Where I differ is with his drawing solely upon his theatrical training and experience, to help him teach others how to better communicate. Not everyone has Alda's theatrical experience.

However, rather than acting (although there are degrees of improvisational acting in many fields), my vocation was university teaching, where, admittedly I often improvised. Yet, as a professor emeritus at San Jose State University, my method of communicating was to draw on material from other writers, educators, and communicators.

Using a disciplined approach to communication problems, MIT sociologist and clinical psychologist Sherry Turkle argues that a human relational problem exists in our culture, one shared by everyone, yet which drives a seemingly impenetrable wedge between us all. That problem is the lack of *real* conversation.

As many in today's society can recognize, it is almost as if the smartphone and other "smart" technologies are creating a new atmosphere. Turkle suggests in *Reclaiming Conversation: The Power of Talk in a Digital Age* that people are trading interpersonal human communication for technological connectivity.

Unlike text messages that pass digitally between people, dialogue is meaningful speech between two or more people; it is meaningful because of speech's emotive pauses and innovative gestures which invite empathic listening and responsible responding. Impossible to be repeated by thumbing letters, a genuine interhuman dialogue requires the presence of mutuality with another person.

What's missing in text messaging, for instance, is facial tone, ironic expression, anger, rhetorical intention and subtle disbelief. But even more, what's lacking are occasions of self-doubt and self-questioning. These are necessary to glimpse if the other is to receive the fullness of one's message.

---

3. Ibid., 195.

What's missing in digital messaging, it seems to me, is the ability that face-to-face dialogue allows us to relate mutually to one another.

How different it is when persons who talk to one another are reciprocally involved with each other, instead of remaining on their own side of the conversation. Smartphones and social media encourage a monologue-like form of expression. Never before has there been a greater need for more open-communication between and among peoples, organizations, and cultures.

Strangely enough, another well-known writer to address our communications breakdown, our misunderstandings of one another, is theoretical physicist David Bohm. He argues in his well-known work, *On Dialogue*, that when dialogue is genuine, especially in a dialogue group (whole person to whole person) a different kind of consciousness is possible—a *participatory consciousness*. According to Bohm, *that's* what is missing—each person's participation in the dialogical process.

The object of dialogue, according to Bohm, is not to analyze, argue, or exchange opinions. Rather, in dialogue, one person shares a point of view, another adds to it, another enhances it. Together, we share in a new type of consciousness. Bohm writes that we share:

> A common content, even if we don't agree entirely. It may turn out that the opinions are not really very important—they are all assumptions. And if we can see them all, we may then move more creatively in a different direction. We can just simply share the appreciation of the meanings; and out of this, whole things, truth emerges unannounced—not that we have chosen it.[4]

In Bohm's brief book, more like an extended essay, the reader is left with unanswered questions, questions like: What happens when people don't realize the necessity of the dialogical process? And while there are no rules for dialogue, as Bohm affirms, there are principles. But what are these principles and how are they to be applied and integrated?

For answers to questions like these, we will turn our full attention for engaging in dialogue to the philosophical anthropologist Martin Buber.

If a failure of communication is a main cause of difficulties we are experiencing in society, it is no surprise that this book is about dialogue and what makes dialogue genuine. What may be surprising, however, is that this book utilizes a philosophical approach rather than a psychological, social-scientific, or communications one.

4. Bohm, *On Dialogue*, 30.

Many of our loftiest ideals—like civility or dialogue—seem to be demonstrably straight-forward, until the moment we try to define them when their complex tensions are revealed. It was in this spirit that the European philosopher, Martin Buber (1878-1965), attempted early in the twentieth century, to pin down the true meaning of the term, "dialogue."

Buber believed dialogue to be our human birthright, the quality that allows us to attain our innate self-realization, and to overcome individualizing squabbles through the dynamics of co-creative togetherness. Dialogue requires, in Buber's estimation, a person's openness to and practice of four constitutive elements, each gathering others together with communal purpose.

Structure

This narrative, which is bracketed by an Introduction and a Conclusion, is broken into three parts. Its Introduction portrays the profoundly necessary story of Buber's conversion from mysticism to dialogue. This is really a shift from trying to live outside the world to being justified simply by living in the world, through one's ever-new response to the fullness of the moment. Buber's conversion bears witness to what Buber will eventually come to call "the life of dialogue, the primal ground of all that is true and creative."[5]

Martin Buber, one of the world's most distinguished and profoundly creative thinkers of the twentieth century, famously argued that the fundamental fact of human existence is person with person and that practicing genuine dialogue was necessary for anyone who wished to become authentically human. There it is! The first two parts of this book seek to unleash and reassemble the core elements for practicing dialogue—turning and addressing, then listening and responding. The book's central thesis is: the innermost growth of the self, despite what many people say, does *not* come in relation to one's self. Rather, attaining one's authentic human existence emerges again and again through genuine dialogue, or in the realm of "participatory consciousness." We become authentically human in and through our relationships with others.

Buber's Dialogue thus includes four distinct but inseparable moments.

---

5. Buber, *Martin Buber*, 24.

Core Elements/Practices of Genuine Dialogue

Turning: Reorienting your focus from self to others as dialogical partners through making them fully present, and being made present by them.

Addressing: Willingly accepting, affirming, and confirming the other as a dialogical partner, even if disagreeing with their convictions.

Listening: Deeply and attentively to the other's speaking and boldly (empathically) swinging to their side by imagining their wholeness and unity.

Responding: Responsibly answering another's communication by trusting that they, like you, will respond honestly and vulnerably.

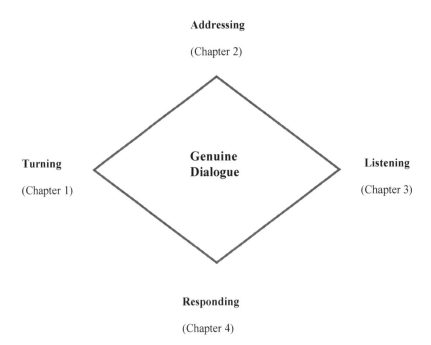

The inaugural Part focuses on Readiness, preparatory practices initiating real dialogue: *Turning* (Chapter 1) and *Addressing* (Chapter 2). Part II focuses on Interactions supporting real dialogue: *Listening* (Chapter 3), and *Responding* (Chapter 4), that take us deeply into the heart of dialogue. These four theory-based principles/practices have been derived through constant repetition over time. Taken together, they create a sense of wholeness, an experience of coherence. Part III, then focuses on Exemplifications: an interview-dialogue with Zen Buddhist, Kobun Chino Roshi (Chapter 5), and one with world renowned philosopher of dialogue, and Buber expert, Maurice Friedman (Chapter 6).

Turning (Chapter 1) is quintessential. Without mutual turning, there is no dialogue. Turning refers to a double movement: away from all self-preoccupations and distractions and completely, unreservedly toward the other. It is this pivot of one's attention fully toward the other that opens up the dialogic path. *Turning* occurs when at least one of the dialogical partners reorients their direction of movement away from the self and fully (body/mind/spirit) toward the other. Genuine dialogue becomes a possibility when we are able to suspend our focus from what we are doing to the other person's interests and intentions. It is almost as simple as changing your physical position so that you are more able to shift your body into a direct face-to-face encounter with the other person.

Addressing (Chapter 2) takes *turning* further. It involves the art of becoming fully respectful of the other and in the process of opening up the space for the other to become fully present to you. *Addressing* occurs when each of the dialogue partners cooperatively accepts the personhood of the other, and then no matter race or culture, gender, age, health or handicap, affirms the other's right to their own opinions, viewpoints, attitudes, or beliefs, even when different from one's own. We address one another through meaningful speech in which we honestly present ourselves.

The second Part focuses on relational practices. By *listening* (Chapter 3) Buber does not just mean active listening. Far deeper, dialogic listening includes the ability to empathically swing to the other's side and think, feel, and experience what they are thinking, feeling, and experiencing. *Listening* occurs when each of the dialogue partners hear cooperatively and listen deeply to what is actually said, as well as silences and pauses. Listening is aided by a simple question: "Did you mean that?" Or, "Would you please say what you just said in a different way?" Or, "Is this what you mean?"

Responding (Chapter 4) is the fruition of the process. Nothing is withheld. One engages the other both responsibly and honestly, courageously risking one's self-image, creatively asking inventive questions, and curiously following provocative leads. *Responding* occurs when each of the partners cooperatively answers the other person by taking a stand, by speaking in a responsible way honestly, courageously, and without leaving anything out.

Part III then provides two exemplifications: two interview-dialogues on death and dying. The first (Chapter 5) is with Japanese Zen Teacher, Kobun Chino Roshi, who was at one time my teacher in Santa Cruz, California. He taught both Zazen (seated Zen), and Dharma (enlightenment discourse). The dialogue was taken from a transcript of an exchange between us at San Jose State University in my "Death, Dying, and Religions" class. The dialogue is direct, blunt, minimalist, open-hearted, and honest. I can imagine end-of-life caregivers being drawn to what Kobun says.

Part III concludes (Chapter 6) with an interview-dialogue with Professor Maurice Friedman. From him, I learned about the internationally known philosopher of dialogue, Martin Buber. Friedman's interview, conducted at his dining room table in Solana Beach, California, is also about death and dying, yet it offers quite a different perspective than Kobun's. This interview was extremely interesting to me in as much as it both reminded me how much I learned from him, and of places where I have come to differ. One of my favorite moments is when he responds to a question about "what's missing from our usual responses to questions about one's dying?"

Practicing

The goal, the challenge in this book is to describe by illustrating and illustrate by describing the practice of genuine dialogue. For this reason, each chapter includes illustrative stories of the specific element being described as well as an analytical description of that element, and commentary on the challenges and breakthroughs that open up for us. Because of the constant interweaving of narrative and analysis, *Martin Buber's Dialogue: Discovering Who We Really Are* is rescued from either a dry, dispassionate historical tone, or the over-simplification of complexities in Buber's thought.

Rather than crafting another historical and philosophical interpretation of Buber's life-work (writings and teachings), this book stands out for at least two reasons: 1) it distinguishes the inestimable value of *genuine dialogue* between persons grasped by an innate self-realization and the dynamics of a reciprocal togetherness; and 2) it challenges us to the all-the-time necessity of *practicing* its foundational elements (turning, addressing, listening, responding).

More than remembering these elements, as if to answer an exam question, practicing their liberating interactions ignites genuine dialogue's co-creative fruitfulness, which is found nowhere else. Practicing these four elements engenders the dialogue process and enables our authentic existence to emerge. And while there's no right way to practice genuine dialogue, here is what's deeply intriguing: the best teacher, the finest coach for learning the art of practicing genuine dialogue is practice itself. No finer mentor exists than the very thing one wants to learn, that is by doing exactly what practicing needs you to do.

It could very well be, and this is my experience, that the more I practice genuine dialogue, the more I am chosen by it—chosen by its meanings, chosen by its participatory consciousness—the more I am granted the graceful pleasure of communicating authentically. If I say to you, this practice has altered my life, it would be because, although I didn't always get what I wanted, by practicing genuine dialogue, I certainly got what I needed.

Acknowledgments

ALBERT EINSTEIN BELIEVED IN "a beautiful and mysterious order underlying the world." Martin Buber, Einstein's dear friend, characterized "genuine dialogue" as the "beautiful and mysterious order" underlying all interhuman endeavors. It is here where we stand. How grateful I am for those I encounter on the narrow ridge.

For Katy Bussell, my snowboarding typist who, between snow and university studies typed the first draft of this manuscript, but not only that, she recognized and corrected typos; but not only that, she helped me smooth out bumpy sentences along the way. Katy was always ready, always timely, always dialogical, always learning. A psychology major, she was gifted with empathic listening with responsible responding—enough to justify attentive respect.

For Rose Meredith Tracey Kramer, my mother, who never gave me a single reason not to trust her unconditionally, who from my earliest childhood taught me—by living it—the virtue, the pleasure of practicing genuine dialogue. There would be no reason for her to read this book, though I would like nothing more, nothing, because she thoroughly embodied dialogue.

For Roy Paul Kramer, my father, who bequeathed me with what my closest friend in graduate school called "fidelity to the task," or my mother once said, "Like your father, you always finish what you start."

For, as always, my daughters, Leila and Yvonne, who not only continue to encourage me, but continue to challenge and question why I write what I write. Yes, for my daughters to whom I dedicate everything I do, who allowed me to raise them as a single parent, and in the process, raised me as a fastidiously fit father. The book turns the wheel of love around and round for you girls, for you.

For my son-in-law, Aaron, a gourmet cook, who every day brews a fresh pot of organic coffee for family and friends, which enlivens my writer's mind and quickens my innovative imagination for the project at hand; and for Ritch, my other son-in-law, whose expertise keeps my specially adapted vehicle rocking and rolling.

For my grandchildren: Sienna Rose, at eight, and Grayson Paul, almost six, that each of you at the right time will remember, or be reminded, that this is the book grandpa was always working on at his desk as you ran circles around me while I continued writing and saying, "I hope beyond hope that when you can read, when you are older, you'll discover the better-than-ice-cream taste of *Buber's Dialogue*.

For Professor Martin Buber, for providing us with the basic elements of genuine dialogue, the practice of which draws us closer to family, friends, and strangers around the world and who thereby enables the treasure hidden in our midst, our authentic self-being to emerge.

For Professor Maurice Friedman, my dissertation advisor, and the person who, more than anyone, taught me the inestimable value of Buber's writings and teachings, and who, toward the end of his life, honored me by inviting me to write the Foreword to his final Buber book, *My Friendship with Martin Buber*.

For Robert C. Morgan, an original friend since we met in 1963—imagine him playing his guitar while driving his green VW Bug at night along Storrow Drive, with the windows open and us singing freedom songs. His friendship has only deepened and widened over the years. I especially wanted a non-Buber expert (Professor Morgan is an internationally known painter, art historian, and author of *The End of the Art World*) to write the Foreword, so as to address readers with an eclectic perspective. He honors me by bringing his expertise to this project even though, get this, he says I honor him.

For Charlie McDowell, professor of computer science at University of California, Santa Cruz who willingly agreed to step outside his field, way outside, to read the entire manuscript, making helpful comments, and most importantly, challenging me with intelligent questions that had to be addressed in the manuscript.

For Ziggy, who enthusiastically encouraged me to complete this project and then read through the complete document, making notes in appropriate places, all before leaving to visit Japan. I can only hope this book becomes for readers as her book of poetry, *The Gate of Our Coming and Going,* became for me.

For Mechthild Gawlick, a dialogical friend along the way who grew up in Germany in a family where the teachings of Martin Buber were read and discussed, and with whom I always discuss Buber's important German terms. Though she disagrees ("we each teach each other"), she has taught me more than I have taught her.

For Nancy Krody, who over the years has copy edited articles and explorations before they were published in *The Journal of Ecumenical Studies* where she is managing editor. Gracefully, she agreed to bring her invaluable expertise to this text so that it now reads more smoothly, more seamlessly—freshened by the Nancy Krody touch.

For my former students: "I apologize that I wasn't able to better understand and better be able to express these principles when we were together in class. To the future students/readers: to you I pass on a transformational tool that continues to rescue me from becoming stuck with/in myself." Thank you.

For the multicolored universe as she manifests herself in my large yard into which I have gazed countless times with an opened mind through the seasons of writing this book. For the calla lilies and birds of paradise, the begonias and daffodils in spring's announcement of this new book's completion.

And for the creative process itself: for inspiration, or better, for what creates ideas within and between persons; for the space, the place, from which the main as well as auxiliary ideas arise without which there would be no book.

For all readers who temporarily set aside disbelief and distractions, and who willingly read the book, as Buber suggests, dialogically.

Introduction

JUST AS THE SUN finally broke through the morning fog, sending it back to the Pacific Ocean, I was sitting attentively listening and conversationally speaking with a dear friend. She was telling me about being apprehensive when thinking about a friend of hers with whom she recently had a disagreement. She was anxious because she knew she needed to take a stand against her friend, but wasn't sure how best to do it.

Before leaving her house, she spoke with her husband who was in the process of restoring an antique vehicle. Having watched him successfully restore cars over the years, and in light of what she was about to do, she asked him: "How do you decide where to begin fixing the engine?"

"That's the most important question you can ask yourself before beginning," he said to her with a playfully devilish smirk.

"That's why I'm asking you," she said with an equally playful hand on her hip.

At that, he paused. He could tell how serious she was. "First of all," he said, "it's important to take time before you begin to discern the best way to begin. Then, the form you take will follow the way in which you begin."

As I was beginning to write this introduction, I recalled that conversation. Suddenly I wondered, could it be that I too am trying to restore an antique engine of sorts? Instead of a car that runs on gasoline and takes you from place to place, am I trying to restore the meaning, value, and significance of an antique process, that of "genuine dialogue," which takes you from place to place on the road of mutuality? And if so, how should I begin?

Meeting Buber

Unquestionably the hero and driving force of this narrative, Martin Buber—one of the world's most profound and creative philosophers of the twentieth century—needs a proper introduction. While I may not be the best person to provide it, let me try through these personal episodes. Actually, if you were to hear either of the following two events separately—1) the story of my teacher Maurice Friedman's discovery, meeting, and becoming the one who single-handedly popularized Martin Buber in America; and 2) the story of my meeting Maurice Friedman, who became my teacher, mentor, and dissertation advisor in a literature and religion graduate program, where I mainly studied not Martin Buber but T. S. Eliot—you might shake your head in disbelief. But, instead of keeping these stories separate, this Introduction combines them to portray the way their double unbelievability reversed itself, and in the process, completely turned my life around when my teacher's teacher also became mine.

When Friedman first met Buber in 1951 in a New York hotel, Buber welcomed him by taking his hand and looking deeply into his eyes. Buber was so full of life from within, an effervescence shined through his face. Friedman's initial response was to feel how totally "other" Buber seemed. His eyes were of a depth, gentleness, and directness that Friedman had never before, or since, encountered.[1]

For this reason, in 1961, a year after Friedman had spent four months in Jerusalem with Buber, he asked himself, "What did I experience when I looked into Buber's eyes?" Upon reflection, Friedman realized that when he looked into Buber's eyes, he understood that Buber really included him and, for this very reason, also placed a demand on him to be fully present. As Friedman indicates, this was by no means an easy demand!

But let's back up a minute. I first met Martin Buber through his lyrical classic, *I and Thou* (1923/57) in an undergraduate philosophy class. One day in class, the professor introduced Martin Buber, an Austrian-born, Israeli philosopher of dialogue, saying that for Buber, "genuine dialogue" (present, direct, and two-sided) existed not only between people but also between people and nature.

He then read a passage from *I and Thou* in which Buber speaks of entering into an I-Thou/You relationship with a tree—a tree! While we normally relate to trees as objects of our perception, as a problem for builders, or as

---

1. Friedman, *Encounter on the Narrow Ridge*, 334.

a source of wood, there is another way to know a tree: as a You, as a unique other. The professor then read: "Everything belonging to the tree, its form and structure, its colors and chemical composition, its intercourse with the elements and with the stars, are all present in a single whole."[2]

Five years later I met Buber a second time. I would return to Temple University (after studying theology and literature, and then teaching for a year) to begin my PhD in Religion and Literature. And who turned out to be my major professor? Maurice Friedman. Unknown to me at the time, it was Friedman who almost single-handedly introduced the work of Martin Buber in the United States with his translations of many of Buber's books and articles and through his groundbreaking book about all of Buber's then-known publications, *Martin Buber: The Life of Dialogue* (1955).

Nor did I know it was Friedman's understanding and expression of Buber's writings that led Buber to comment: "To systemize a wild-grown thought as mine is, without impairing its elementary character seem to me a remarkable achievement. On a rather multifarious work Dr. Friedman has not imposed an artificial unity; he has disclosed the hidden one."[3]

One day—can you believe it?—after deciding to write my dissertation on T. S. Eliot, in response to a student's question in a "literature and existentialism" class about human authenticity, Friedman told us that five days before he first met Buber, Buber first met T. S. Eliot in London, before coming to America. Friedman told us:

> ... while Eliot was a shy man, he had a frankness that Buber really liked. I tried to draw [Buber] out further by asking him whether he did not find that his opinions differed from Eliot's in important respects. "When I meet a man," Buber replied, "I am not concerned about his opinions but about the man himself." I took this as a reproof, as indeed it was. In my mind, Buber and Eliot had stopped being real persons and had become chessmen in a dialectical game.[4]

Buber met persons as they are, minus all judgments and suspicions, even if they turn out to be true. Buber's openness startled me. While Friedman took Buber's remark as a reproof, I took it as a challenge, even a calling. How amazing! I knew then that Buber eventually would become my

---

2. Buber, *I and Thou* (trans. Smith), 7–8. All subsequent quotations from *I and Thou* are taken from the Smith translation.

3. Quoted on the back cover of Friedman, *Martin Buber: A Life of Dialogue*.

4. Friedman, *My Friendship with Martin Buber*, 36.

real teacher. Even though it didn't happen immediately, and even though I never personally met Buber, through my teacher, Professor Maurice Friedman, I came to understand that Buber lived what he taught and taught how to live dialogically. Gradually I did too.

And I was fortunate to have Friedman as my mentor. When Buber first read Friedman's doctoral dissertation on him, he was struck by Friedman's thoroughness and seriousness. He sent Friedman all of his works that Friedman did not know and helped him accumulate a comprehensive bibliography. A few years later, when Friedman was writing *Martin Buber: The Life of Dialogue* (1955), Buber patiently answered all of Friedman's questions at full length. Friedman thus had at hand the authentic written explanations of many points at issue.

Then a few years later Friedman would translate a great number of Buber's essays and articles as well as several of his books. It was as if Friedman knew intimately and said what Buber would say when discussing significant viewpoints. For that reason, when Friedman spoke in class or in later years during our friendship, I sometimes felt that I was listening to Buber himself.

It was Buber's understanding of "genuine dialogue" and Friedman's ability to express and explain it that supported my intellectual curiosity. It is in and through genuine dialogue that a person can experience authentic humanness.

What sets Buber apart from most humanist thinkers is that Buber has placed "genuine dialogue"—direct, honest, open, spontaneous, mutual communication—at the center of his intellectual narrative, as well as his life. As Abraham Joshua Heschel, Buber's great friend, remarked shortly before Buber died:

> I know of no one with a life as rich with intellectual adventures or who so strongly responded to their challenges as Martin Buber. His greatest contribution was himself, his very being. There was magic in his personality, richness in his soul. His sheer presence was joy . . . He loved to listen and to talk, and our conversations sometimes lasted twelve to thirteen hours.[5]

Buber was a polyglot (he spoke German, Hebrew, Yiddish, Polish, English, French, and Italian, and read in addition to these, Spanish, Latin, Greek, and Dutch).[6] In response to often asked questions about whether

5. Friedman, *Encounter on the Narrow Ridge*, 459.

6. Ibid., 7.

Buber really lived his philosophy, Friedman indicated: "He walked his talk as people like to say today. He really lived the life of dialogue, and to him it was really 'the only life worth living.'"[7]

How striking, then, that Buber would say with full confidence:

> I do not accept any absolute formulas for living . . . No preconceived code can see ahead to everything that can happen in a [person's] life. As we live, we grow, and our beliefs change. They must change. So I think we could live with this constant discovery. We should be open to this adventure in heightened awareness of living. We should stake our whole existence on our willingness to explore and experience.[8]

If one has been skimming along the surface of these words thus far without really being drawn in by them, drink in Friedman's remarkable description of Martin Buber, as one who "lives what he has written," which is, for Friedman (and certainly for this writer) a more marvelous achievement than his writing itself. In this slice of life, Friedman's observation of Buber's wholeness and humanness is a driving force of the book:

> I have seen him in many different situations and always I have received the same impression of him—a *real* human being interested in this life we all live and in how to hallow just this very life. I have never understood what it means to be a real human being, but Martin Buber has now shown me. He is, second, a religious man, not a spiritual man or a mystic. The difference is very important . . . Finally, I would say about Martin Buber that he is a man to whom one could tell anything about one's life and feel positive that he would not be shocked and he would not judge.
>
> He is a short man, built stickily . . . very imposing with his white beard that makes him look like a prophet. His brown eyes are the most outstanding physical feature he has. I shall never forget the look he gave me when I first met him. I would not call his eyes penetrating, but rather *open*. Sometimes when he looks at you, you feel that you are looking right *into* the man and you feel a sudden great, comforting warmth. He confirms the other person. He smiles and laughs often; often when he smiles, his face has a charming disarmed look. I have several times seen him with a stern look that passed quickly, and he is always serious. This last doesn't bother me at all; in fact, it is a relief to me.

7. Friedman, *My Friendship with Martin Buber,* xviii.

8. Hodes, *Martin Buber,* 56.

I know that Martin Buber has suffered very much, but his suffering has knit him together into a whole human being. Often a suffering human being is like a sick or crippled human being. But not so with him. He turns and responds to human encounter with his whole being in an absolute, consistent steadiness. I heard him say that the teacher's function is 'to give the student trust, just to be there for [them], like a mother is for the child.' This is what Martin Buber does. He gives one trust . . .[9]

I must admit that it wasn't until Friedman was in his eighties, and I had a chance to read the manuscript of his last Buber book, *My Friendship with Martin Buber*, that I discovered another stunning connection between Buber and Friedman. In a letter Buber once wrote, he recommended Friedman for a teaching position at Columbia University. I have read this letter over many times, and again now. Buber's words both link Friedman to his teacher, Buber, and, if I dare say it, my teacher's teacher to myself. Speaking of the power of Friedman's mind, Buber writes:

He understands the ideas he meets, and he understands even the persons who thought them, as persons who thought just these ideas and not different ones. I am sorry to say that he had to do in this case with a somewhat resisting subject, but he succeeded to grasp it adequately. His best faculty is to express and to explain what he has understood . . . I have the impression that I have told you what perhaps no other could tell you about the man. It is because for all these years I have been a witness and now I have come to give evidence.[10]

Buber and Friedman: Friedman and Buber. In this book I have done my best to truly *understand, express*, and *explain* my teacher's teacher's teaching as well as understanding the person who thought just these ideas and not other ones.

Human Birthright

Does it makes sense that some of life's most powerfully important lessons can take a lifetime to learn? Not so for Martin Buber. As a young man, he

9. I have taken this quotation from an email Prof. Friedman sent me in 2009, which he said was taken from his written draft of a book which eventually became *My Friendship with Martin Buber*.

10. Friedman, *My Friendship with Martin Buber*, 98.

learned one of the most significant lessons of his life—namely, that "genuine dialogue" is our human birthright, the common human denominator that bares ramifications throughout the rest of our life. One of these ramifications is the door this book opens, through which our authentic human existence emerges. By the end of the book, we come to recognize this most powerfully important lesson—our innate self-realization emerges through the opening of elemental togetherness between us.

Buber provides a meaning for the word "dialogue" that is significantly different from the way it is usually used to mean a discussion or exchange of ideas or points of view, especially when persons try to prove their viewpoint. Buber's reference to the etymological derivation deepens its meaning. Dialogue comes from the Greek term *dialogos*. *Logos*, appropriately, has the meaning of "word" or "meaning." And *dia* means "through," or "across," or "between."

For Buber, therefore, *dialogos* suggests speaking meaningful words back and forth between people across an invisible membrane that separates us. Dialogic behavior from Greek culture to the present, is meaningful in itself. Trying to define its significance would be like attempting to define a line of poetry. Impossible. Thus, our first question (the answer to which flows through this little book) is this: What makes dialogue genuine?

It should be understood from the beginning that "dialogue," as Buber used it and as it will be used here, does not refer to you-speak-I-speak exchanges. Nor does it refer to phatic chatter between people. Rather, it refers to what Martin Buber calls "real dialogue": speaking meaningfully and responding responsibly to everyone we meet. To clarify his view, Buber named three realms of dialogue: genuine, technical, and monological.

1. **Genuine Dialogue:** "Whether spoken or silent . . . each of the participants really has in mind the other or the others in their present and particular being and turns to them with the intention of establishing a living mutual relation[ship] between himself and them."

2. **Technical Dialogue:** That communication which is "prompted solely by the need of objective understanding."

3. **Monologue Disguised as Dialogue:** That situation in which "two or more men, meeting in space, speak each with himself in strangely tortuous and circuitous ways and yet imagine they have escaped the torment of being thrown back on their own resources."[11]

11. Buber, *Between Man and Man*, 33.

Dialogue becomes *genuine* when each of the participants is fully present to the other or others, openly attentive to all voices, and willing to be nonjudgmental and vulnerable.

One way we will come to understand what Buber means by genuine dialogue is by coming to discern its center. Where does dialogue exist? The beauty, the simplicity, the invaluable significance of Buber's insightful response to this question fuels this book. The heart center of genuine dialogue cannot be found within one or the other of its participants. Neither does it equal the sum total of their input. Rather, it emerges from the oscillating sphere between and around them. Thereby, according to Buber, dialogue's center is the immediate presence of reciprocal interhuman mutuality among dialogical partners, from which each person's unique identity emerges.

Unlike monologue, in which the speaker only has him or herself in mind, or technical dialogue, in which the speaker solely has the need to communicate objective data in mind, what is it that makes dialogue genuine? Six years after publishing *I and Thou* in 1929, in an essay called "Dialogue," let me repeat Buber's one sentence pointer: the heart of genuine dialogue lies in the fact that "Each of the participants really has in mind the other or others in their present and particular being and turns to them with the intention of establishing a living mutual relation between himself and them."[12] What makes dialogue genuine is when it becomes whole person to whole person, eye-to-eye, voice-to-voice, and gesture-to-gesture communication.

While usually genuine dialogue uses words, words are not necessary. Real dialogue can happen in silence, through looks, glances, and gestures. In rare moments when I wave to a passing friend, it is possible to communicate an entire conversation without words being exchanged.

One hot afternoon in Tokyo, for example, while sitting on a bench waiting for a bus, I looked across the street and saw an elderly man and an elderly woman speaking to one another. He was practically bald; her gray hair was pulled up in a bun. At one point, he bowed deeply to her; she, in turn, bowed deeply to him. He then bowed deeply to her; she, in turn, bowed deeply to him. After repeating this once again, he turned and walked away. She stood there quietly. Then, silently, she bowed again to the empty space in which he had stood. A silent dialogue had just happened.

---

12. Ibid., 13.

From Mysticism to Dialogue

First, before considering any of Buber's writings and teachings about dialogue, it would be helpful to discuss what he himself later called a "conversion" event. The word "conversion" is normally used in a religious context—a reorientation from a fully secular life to a fully religious one. Not so for Buber; in fact, almost the opposite—from a life of mystical rapture to one of everyday dialogue. Buber realized a fully religious life could not in any way be separated from the fullness of ordinary life, lived in the way it presents itself.

If as Buber wrote, "All real living is meeting," mismeeting, on the other hand, thwarts dialogue.[13] Consider differences: mismeeting occurs when one dismisses the other, misrecognizes the other, and therefore miscommunicates with the other. Real meeting occurs when one accepts the other, affirms the other, and confirms the other.

In Buber's mid-30s, as World War I was breaking out, one morning in 1914, after hours of ecstatic rapture, he received a visit from a troubled young student without himself being fully present. He was still partly distracted by his morning's mystical fervor, in which his self was temporarily lost in the all-self.

Buber had a pleasant conversation with the young man. He often was visited by students and carried on a fairly typical conversation with him. "Only," Buber later confessed, "I omitted to imagine the questions he did not ask."[14] Incredible!

Buber learned from a friend that the young visitor had come to him not for a casual chat, but for help to make a life-decision. The student went to the front line and was killed, as Buber later writes, "out of despair which did not oppose his own death."[15] Imagine how powerfully regenerative Buber's empathic ability was: to be able to enter into the other person's consciousness, and be able to sense what the other was thinking and feeling.

Buber experienced the news of the visitor's death as a judgment to which he responded by shifting the axis of his behavior from seeking inner-realizations to participating in interhuman ones. "Since then," Buber continues:

13. Buber, *I and Thou*, 11.
14. Buber, *Meetings*, 10–11.
15. Martin Buber, in a letter to Maurice Friedman.

I have given up the "religious," which is nothing but the exception, extraction, exaltation, ecstasy; or it has given me up. I possess nothing but the everyday, out of which I am never taken. The mystery is no longer disclosed, it has escaped or it has made its dwelling here where everything happens where it happens. I know no fullness but each mortal hour's fullness of claim and responsibility. Though far from being equal to it, yet I know that in the claim I am claimed and may respond in responsibility, and know who speaks and demands a response.[16]

Amazingly clear, brilliantly direct, Buber portrays a movement from *that* (inner exulted ecstasy) to *this* (moment-by-moment claim and responsibility). As Maurice Friedman writes:

Thus, Buber gave up the much more perfect and satisfying fullness of mystic rapture, in which the self experiences no division within or limit without, for the always imperfect fullness of the common world of speech-with-meaning built up through ever-demanding, ever-painful meetings with others. Not expansion of consciousness to the All but awareness of otherness, not universality but uniqueness, not perfection but the unreduced immediacy of the 'lived concrete,' became Buber's way of life from this time on.[17]

I repeat part of Buber's remarkable statement: "I possess nothing but the everyday, out of which I am never taken. The mystery is no longer disclosed, it has escaped or it has made its dwelling here where everything happens . . . where I am claimed and respond in responsibility."

Surprisingly, at first glance, but less so after you ponder it, Buber continues:

I do not know much more. If that is religion then it is just *everything* simply all that is lived in its possibility of dialogue. Here is the space also for religion's highest forms. As when you pray you do not thereby remove yourself from this life of yours but in your praying refer your thought to it, even though it may be in order to yield . . . this moment is not extracted from [life], it rests on what has been and beckons to the remainder that has still to be lived: You are not swallowed up in a fullness without obligation, you are willed for the life of communion.[18]

---

16. Buber, *Meetings*, 46.
17. Friedman, *Encounter on the Narrow Ridge*, 81.
18. Buber, *The Letters of Martin Buber*, 45–46.

Buber points here to an often overlooked double-conversion—both religious and dialogical. Buber's awakening—from mysticism to dialogue, from self-possessed feelings to other-directed attention, from the "false" self to the "real" self—transformed the rest of his life. No matter what came his way, instead of dreading it, or resisting it, he faced it with an open-minded dialogical attitude.

First, he remarked, as a result of the young man's visit, along with his inadequate response, he gave up the "religious," the exceptional, the ecstatic, the rapturous, the mysterious, gave it up for the everyday in which we are ever set. Second, he gave up the dialogical, if by that one means nothing more than phatic chatter or casual chit-chat. He gave up non-genuine dialogue for presence-to-presence, moment-by-moment mutual speaking and responding.

The triggering problems arose when Buber received the young man without *turning* wholeheartedly away from his morning's rapture and toward the young visitor, and without *listening* deeply to what was being said, and what was left unsaid. Reflecting on the incident, Buber later realized that the very dialogue he was being called into—"the fullness of claim and responsibility"—enabled authentic human existence to emerge between persons in genuine dialogue.

To the extent that Buber brought his early mystical proclivities along with him into his life of dialogue, it was a mysticism of the particular, of ordinary life events. This was especially true of Taoism (breathing is Taoism), Zen Buddhism (walking is Zen; sitting is Zen), and eighteenth century Hasidism (hallowing the everyday is Hasidism).

Notice: in the teaching of the Tao, the Tao only becomes actual and manifest through the perfected person's contact with the world of particulars, with stones and water, with earth and air. In the popular communal mysticism of eighteenth-century Hasidism, a disciple once asked his teacher, "What was the most important thing for your teacher?" to which he said: "Whatever he appeared to be doing at that moment." Buber compared these sayings to a Zen disciple's question of his teacher: "What is the word, the action that wipes out the sin of millions of eons," to which the Zen master's answer was, "What is right under your nose!"[19] These mysticisms of the particular continued to enrich Buber's ever-developing nondoing doing practice of living dialogue authentically.

19. Friedman, *Martin Buber and the Eternal*, 121.

Dialogical Interpretation

I say all this to indicate that my third, fourth, and future meetings with Buber occurred each time I returned to encounter his writings, usually to quote him in a project I was working on or to refresh my memory about something Buber said.

Buber would suggest, and this is what fully attracts me to his writings, that the appropriate way to read a text (like this one) is to hear its voice, to discover its meaning not within yourself, but between yourself and the text in dialogue. The power of Buber's words, phrases, images, idiosyncrasies, and metaphors draws readers into meaningful dialogues with his text (intensifying our awareness of its meaning).

Herein lays my utter fascination with Buber's dialogical motive for and method of reading. Essentially, according to Buber, a text becomes person-like by virtue of its unique personal address, which is understood in a back-and-forth conversational movement. Thus, meaning does not originate in the reader's senses as he or she responds to the text, but arises in the oscillating realm of the *between*, whose interaction embraces the whole being of both text and reader. I meet Buber anew each time I read him.

In thus engaging and being engaged, the reader encounters the writer's words immediately in the present, as if hearing the voice of the author by turning receptively toward the speaker with one's whole attention, and receiving and responding to the indivisible wholeness of living words.

Therefore, through dialogical interpretation: what I discover about the world and myself is always rediscovered and animated anew; reading texts open-mindedly and responsibly, a dialogical reader discovers and responds to links between his or her personal life and textual insights and recognitions.

The activity of reading dialogically is pictured here taking place in a three-dimensional conversational field which involves reciprocal and reciprocating dialogues: between author and text, author and reader, and reader and text. A text, as visualized here, is not just a soliloquy or a monologue, nor a merely subjective interpretation. Rather, fruitful reciprocities are manifest between voices of the reader and voices of the author through the text.

Dialogical Interpretation

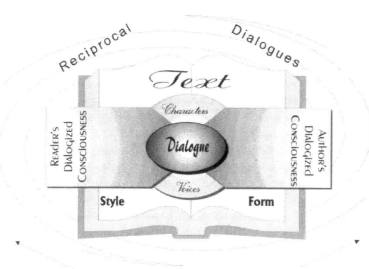

Through a dialogical lens, readers/you can discover and respond to Buber's images of the human vis-à-vis the way you see yourself. What voices do you hear speaking through you? What do you hear inviting and challenging you to consider, as if for the first time? By relating to texts as if personal speech to you, new insights emerge, fresh challenges are felt.

Pointing the Way

Buber once said that even though he remained a philosopher for life, he was an atypical one. As he said of himself:

> I have no teaching. I only point to something . . . I point to something in reality that had not or had too little been seen. I take him who listens to me by the hand and lead him to the window. I open the window and point to what is outside. I have no teaching, but I carry on a conversation.

If one hopes for a teaching from Buber that is anything other than a "pointing," a direction of movement, then one will be disappointed. Rather than a philosophical worldview, his writings are dialogical responses to situations and thinkers he has encountered and one specifically that occurs between Buber and his readers.

What Buber points to, what this book points to, is those who carry on genuine conversations throughout his life. Buber felt duty-bound to bring "decisive experiences" into the "human interference of thought . . . as insight, valid and important for others." Indeed, Buber referred to himself as "a trustworthy elaborator" who was committed to the task of explaining "attained insights," emerging from both personal experiences and interpersonal interactions.[20]

This book aims at being an effective blueprint for pointing to the revival of genuine dialogical communion, offering breakthrough teachings for humanizing our lives. What all this finally comes to is simple and direct: The sought-for treasure, the fulfillment of human existence, can be found right here in the midst of genuine dialogue.

I remember discussing these ideas of rearranging Buber's material on dialogue with Professor Maurice Friedman. "Buber would encourage you," he said to me, "to offer your representations of his material, especially if it brings clarification. I was fortunate," Friedman said, referring to himself, "to be able to ask Buber myself for his opinions. But you know enough about Buber's work to be able to achieve what you're attempting."

My hope is that by unleashing and then reframing Buber's words, relations of parts to the whole, will be brought alive in a new way, and along the way you too will come alive here where you are with others.

20. Martin Buber in Schilpp ed. of *Philosophy of Martin Buber*, 694.

PART I

Readiness

Chapter 1: **Turning**

Clear Skies

The Journey

Turn, Turn, Turn

Reflexion (Bending Back
on Oneself)

Breaking Through Thinking

Tuning In

Meditation to Mutuality

Pivoting Around

Practicing Turning

Chapter 2: **Addressing**

Back from Italy

Accepting and Affirming

Speaking Ever-New

The Orange-Haired Mortician

"A Great Man," T. S. Eliot Said

"There Are No Great Men,"
Buber Said

Making (The Other) Present

Addressing Students

Practicing Addressing

›

1

Turning

Clear Skies

IT WAS A DAY when the skies were clear. Squawking birds flew into a gentle wind current. From the hill on which the University sits, we could see sparkling blues of the Monterey Bay.

After exercising, showering, and dressing inside the gym locker room, I noticed a young man whom I had not seen before. He was tall and handsomely proportioned. His face was quiet, and he appeared self-contained, as if he was completely at ease with his current state of affairs. He too had finished dressing and was gathering his exercise equipment into his bag. We caught each other's eyes at the same moment.

He was standing at one end of a row of lockers; I was sitting at the other end. Wanting to start a conversation, I turned toward him and asked, "What are you studying?"

Immediately, he set his bag down, and turned from the doorway to focus on me. Without being distracted by my limitations, he smiled and said, "I'm an exchange student from the Netherlands. I'm taking General Education classes."

"Sweet deal," I blurted, as a former professor who knew well the difference between General Education and major classes. "You're lucky to get to do that here in California."

He smiled, shaking his head in agreement at the obvious coup he was achieving—receiving transferable General Education credits at University of California, Santa Cruz in Santa Cruz.

"I hope you're also able to take some courses in your major field."

"Yes," he said, "I'm also taking courses in technology."

Standing tall, he talked in a mannered way. His thorough willingness to attentively listen and willingness to speak responsively captured my full attention.

"Your English is impeccable," I said, congratulating him. "I admire both your speaking, your intonation, and your comprehensive grasp of the language."

When I used the slang descriptor "spot on," I interrupted myself to wonder out loud, "Did you understand my use of the slang 'spot on'?"

"Yes," he said, "I speak a lot with English speakers."

Remembering that I had once known a Dutch girl who was also a transfer student, I asked, "Is Meeka a popular Dutch name?"

"I've heard it, yes."

"She once knitted me a sweater," I said as his eyes lit up.

Nodding his head with recognition, "Yes, my grandmother used to do that."

He spoke proudly as he stood tall like the white calla lilies in my yard reaching to the sun. Again, I complimented him on his accent-free spoken English.

"And you've studied other languages, haven't you?" I inquired.

"A little French and German," he said.

"Ah," I said, "can I ask you to translate the following German sentences? According to the philosopher Martin Buber, it's one of the most important ones. It exactly describes what we are doing. 'Alles wirkliche Leben ist Begegnung,' which is from one of his major works."

He shook his head with uncertainty. "Begegnung," I repeated, "is the most significant word in that sentence. It is translated as 'meeting,' or 'encounter,' or 'engagement.' That's what we are doing now."

As I spoke, I extended my left hand first toward him, then I pulled it back toward me: forth and back, back and forth.

"Begegnung is the most important word in the German philosopher Martin Buber's book, I and Thou. It represents his major thesis—that all real living, or actual life is engagement. That's what is happening right now."

He nodded his head in agreement.

"So thank you. By the way, I'm sorry I forgot to ask you: what's your name?"

"Richard," he said smiling as he extended his hand out to me.

"Thank you very much," he said, and, picking up his bag, walked off to class.

The Journey

The span of this story, its itinerary in time and space, represents an assembly of expository commentary and illustrative episodes from notes and dialogical insights released while writing.

The possibility and reality of a dialogical relationship between myself and others—the happening itself—had already captured me in my youth. While spending time with my mother: either sipping Lipton's tea at the kitchen table, or drying dishes, or walking, she—knowing nothing of Martin Buber—taught me dialogical principles by the way she lived, which would reawaken years later. This fundamental interhuman connection, the decisive transformation that takes place in and through authentic dialogue has never abandoned me.

Yet, when I began this journey, dragging my dented authenticity and leaking awareness, I was dogged by doubt. I wouldn't be able to do it, I thought. Why even try? How could I ever write a book that would do justice to Buber's brilliance on the one hand and captivate neophytes to his dialogical technology on the other?

Tracing themes of philosophy, anthropology, myth, ritual, and transcendence, I sought to follow Buber's pioneering theory of "genuine dialogue." I began to engineer the interplay of its fundamental practices. I set innovative references in appropriate historical contexts. Then, with personal interactions added, I began this journey with Buber's dialogue.

How could I ever forget my excitement upon discovering the writings of Martin Buber, writings with power and wisdom for everyday living, writings about how his elevated individualism was shattered by meaningful encounters, openings to respond authentically to the claim and responsibility of each new event, trading selfhood for interrelatedness. Or, as my professor, Maurice Friedman, once wrote:

> Coming to the conviction that the real heart of Buber's philosophy—and of the "lived concrete" about which he was so concerned—is found not in conceptual or systematic thought but in . . . events and meetings[.][1]

How indeed could one ever forget writings so fundamentally transformational? Especially when I came to discover that the word "dialogue," in the context of relationship is what linguists call a "performative utterance"— a word that doesn't simply mean communication or imply back-and-forth

---

1. Buber, *Meetings*, 7.

discourse, but actually *enacts changes.* Dialogue is two or more people actually talking and listening to one another with undivided attention, which causes shifts in behavior.

Looking ahead, aware of where I've been and not wanting to make similar mistakes, the scenes portrayed and discussed here are journeys of discovering the indispensable value of *mutuality,* of mutuality in speech.

Using words like a painter, Buber portrays the emotion and power of dialogue in images like: "vital reciprocity," or "memorable common fruitfulness," or a "dynamic elemental togetherness" these images challenge us to become "We."

But where to start? What to include? What to leave out?

By looking back on Buber's forward-leaning words, we see how his unique description of "genuine dialogue" enables and empowers us to hear each other's voice in situation upon situation, and to respond by making decisions and taking a stand.

Walking along this path: I develop genuine relationships through authentic dialogue; I discover a new identity emerging through the voice of dialogue itself.

"Do you mean this is it? Is this all there is?" I hear myself wondering.

"Well, what else is there?" I say to myself.

"How about trying to know where I am going."

"Where are you going?"

"I'm on the road to find out, you could say."

"And where are you on this road?"

"I'm not sure because it's so difficult to face the past without wondering if that's where I'm headed."

"Is it more important to know exactly where you are heading, or to find out who you are on this path? Isn't that more important than trying to discover where the road is leading you?"

"Yes, no: no, yes. I don't know. I just know I've got to keep going. The world doesn't care."

"Why should it, especially if you're still on the way to finding the one who is looking? Sounds like an impossible conundrum to me. As long as you keep looking around the next corner by yourself, you may perhaps never know."

"Um . . ."

"Time and time again you can find those who can help, not by telling you what to do, but by listening carefully and drawing forth from your dialogical exchange what you would not realize by yourself."

"That sounds too easy, too easy to find my way. Broken moments keep running into me."

"That's true for everyone. No one escapes broken, wounding moments. None of us. The question, therefore, is not what you are going to do, but what We *are* doing."

It took me years and then years more to discover what a transforming effect practicing dialogue can have. Like one's first sip of freshly brewed coffee in the morning, becoming dialogical enlivens the entire situation in which we find ourselves.

Practicing the principles of genuine dialogue (*turning, addressing, listening,* and *responding* to the other) has now become the only possible, plausible, and prolific tool for my life's travels. I say tool as one could say the piano is a tool for enabling magnificent music. Just as striking ivory and ebony keys ignite sounds and singing voices, speaking and listening, listening and responding ignite co-creative voices.

And on my journey, I encountered dialoguing textual voices, and silent articulates, some unwritten thoughts that appeared in white spaces between sections of print. And what did these spaces indicate? Several times I heard: "in a book like this one—a creative nonfiction—make sure to leave elbow room in quiet spaces between chapters and sections which allow breathing room, thinking room, and imagining room for readers to join the creative process." Reading *Martin Buber's Dialogue: Discovering Who We Really Are* is a co-creative event in which you will fill spaces with your own words and images, your own meanings.

To the extent that each of us reveals our self to others in dialogical speech, we hear the Universe speaking in and through us. It is as We, ever again as We that our common speaking has meaning and significance. When our dialogical voices resound together, we discover that We are, in the realest sense, the dialogue itself.

So we arrive at the book's singular pointing, its core finding—not describing "genuine dialogue" (although that does occur), but portraying the inestimable value of *living dialogically,* of practicing its core elements, its independent-interdependent centers of focus, and discovering who we really are.

How could I have not written this book.

Turn, Turn, Turn

"Let's begin with the '60s folk song made popular by The Byrds, "Turn! Turn! Turn!" One could say the book begins here, here where time's purpose is measured by acts of turning. The song gives one the impression that turning itself is time's purpose.

But why here of all places? No real, face-to-face dialogue can occur unless a mutual *turning* fully toward the other occurs. First, it, and it alone, is *the* necessary prerequisite. Each person must re-direct their physical, intellectual, emotional, and spiritual attitudes completely toward the other person.

I can imagine you thinking: "Since the turning must be mutual and since I have no control over the other, what hope is there for genuine dialogue until everyone becomes enlightened?"

Certainly Buber (and I along with him) recognized this most urgent need. That there is mutuality between myself and those with whom I am speaking is as you understand, urgent. However, though I cannot control the other person's "turning," as you can imagine, I have noticed in my own experience that when I model wholeheartedly turning toward the other, and continue to model it, sometimes that modeling is enough to influence the other person to then whole heartedly turn toward me. Beyond that, this subject arises in conversations with people who are interested in possibilities for living a more authentic life. That's perhaps the time when the subject can be best introduced. That is, if and when you are really interested in discussing communication breakdowns that lead to communication breakthroughs, the gateway is necessarily practicing "turning."

Without wholly turning toward the other, genuine dialogue cannot take place. Instead, a technical (exchanging ideas) or monological (talking about yourself to yourself) dialogue occurs. There is, of course, a place for each of these. But to have an authentic dialogue with another person, each person must take the other person fully into consideration.

Turning, reorienting yourself, begins by stopping what you are doing at the moment, and becoming alert to the presence of another person beyond yourself, who has entered your sphere of awareness. They may be a friend or a stranger, family or colleague. The act of turning is both simple, and yet difficult, both a natural expression, and yet needs to be remembered and practiced. Turning is simultaneously an attitude that needs to be maintained throughout the dialogical process, and, as we will discover, practiced in order to become authentic.

So, real dialogue begins as we turn into a relationship with the other person who has also let go of self-oriented interests, to turn fully to you. As you can see, the term *turning* specifies a practice more like an art than like a mystical experience. It refers to radically redirecting one's orientation to life, from self to other in the everyday, every moment world.

Buber contours a radical wholehearted turning as follows:

> In genuine dialogue the turning to the partner takes place in all truth, that is, it is a turning of the being. Every speaker means the partner or partners to whom he turns as this personal existence ... The true turning of his person to the other includes this confirmation, this acceptance. Of course, such a confirmation does not mean approval; but no matter in what I am against the other, by accepting him as my partner in genuine dialogue I have affirmed him as a person.[2]

Let me give words to what I hear you asking. "But why radical?"

For Buber, it should be understood that acts of turning stream through all of the spheres of existence and renew the world. In fact, turning for him is a double movement: first, a turning *away* from everything that would prevent us from entering into a genuine relationship with another; and second, *toward* whoever or whatever presents themselves to us. In other words, the double movement requires turning *away* from self-preoccupation and *toward* entering into relationships. According to Buber, one:

> Who is dominated by the idol that he wishes to win, to hold, and to keep—possessed by a desire for possession—has no way . . . [forward] but that of turning, which is a change, not only of goal, but also of the nature of [a person's] movement.[3]

But what does it mean that we are called to change our inner attitudes by turning? We are called to swing away from being doubled-back upon ourselves. This means changing our very self-orientation. For example: when we are "possessed by a desire for possession," we become immersed in the world of things.

Overcoming this involves a double movement: Turning away from self-affirming interests, narratives, assumptions, thoughts, away from distractions,

2. Buber, *The Knowledge of Man*, 85.

3. Buber, *I and Thou*, 105.

appearances, and impositions; turning toward the other by "temporarily suspending" one's own attitudes and beliefs, by openly surrendering into relationships with the other (person, nature, animal, art, music . . .).

A double movement involves both *distance* (separation, or giving up self-asserting attitudes and abandoning monological forms of discourse) and *relationship* (entering into the presence of the other). Buber realized that turning involves surrendering into the relationship between yourself and the other. It involves letting go (if only temporarily) of whatever you may bring into the present.

Authentic surrender, or letting go of control, occurs only when all self-conscious reflection is temporarily suspended. You'll notice that the surrendering of which Buber speaks does not mean becoming blank or empty-minded, but rather becoming more alive, more present, more open to interacting with others. Turning toward and surrendering into the present teaches us the art of letting go of our need to be in control.

Reflexion (Bending Back on Oneself)

There is, it should be said, a lot that gets in the way of truly turning. Bookshelves are stacked full of "what to do" suggestions. Not that *turning* is easy or automatic. There are distractions, many distractions.

The opposite of turning, Buber writes, is "reflexion," bending back on oneself, as not having the other in mind in his or her otherness and particularity. This backward-bending movement privileges self-consciousness and withdrawal from entering into relationships with others. In other words, by allowing the other to exist only within my own experience, the heart of what is most human gets lost and dissipated. This happens when I turn my experience inward.

In a letter that Buber once sent to Friedman, Buber wrote:

> There are three degrees of reflexion: (1) the indispensable reflecting on my inner (introspective) experience; (2) a centralizing self-attention ("I and my world"); and (3) the elaboration of otherness. According to Friedman, Buber had intended to clarify this in his anthropology but never did so. It seems to me I have made a little discovery," he wrote in asking if I knew any books on the subject, "but it is not easy to express it."[4]

4. Friedman, *My Friendship with Martin Buber*, 81.

I admit that turning toward the other—fully, not partially or incompletely—at first was not easy for me. At times, it's still difficult. Many of us have a built-in orientation to turning back toward ourselves. The opposite of turning—reflexion—remains self-centered, self-preoccupied, self-oriented.

Perhaps because it is so easy to slip back into self-centeredness, turning is an essential feature for me to continually practice.

For instance, a friend comes by for a visit. At the same time, I am at my desk working on something that's very important to me (like this book, for instance). I am given an immediate existential choice: do I or don't I? Do I drop what I'm doing and welcome my visitor into the open space of dialogue, or do I hide behind the excuse of being busy? I often encounter this temptation.

"What are the limits to dialogue," I once asked Professor Friedman in a class at San Jose State University. His response is worth thinking through:

> There are several limits: one is time; one is hunger; and one is that you do what you can in a situation. There are even tragic situations where there are simply not enough resources on either side for a genuine meeting to take place. You don't insist on the dialogue and you don't assume it will always happen—you are simply open to it. If I could make dialogue happen, that wouldn't be dialogue. That would be willfulness. So I have my radius. I can prevent it, though. There can be a one-sided prevention of dialogue. I can do it simply by saying—"nothing's going to get through to me." But when there's a *willingness* for dialogue, then—and you used the word earlier—one must "navigate" moment-by-moment. It's a listening process.

It first must be understood that turning occurs with one's *whole-being*, with all of one's faculties. This whole-hearted action corresponds to the fact that turning is a life-long activity. At the same time, turning is an uneasy practice whose goal is to become spontaneously unthinking, unthinkingly spontaneous.

Every time we meet someone (friend or stranger, family or friend's family) Buber calls us to reorient ourselves away from self-absorption and self-concern to become fully attentive to the other. Away from self, toward others; toward others, away from self. However, instead of turning wholly toward the other, dialogue is prevented, as we have seen, by acts of reflexion. One bends back upon oneself in monologue:

- The other exists only as a portion of my own experience;
- I choose to remain a self-contained, individualized intelligence;
- I refuse to stop what I am doing in order to swing my attention to the other;
- I am unaware of the possibility of becoming "we";
- I am easily distracted by distractions;
- I am only interested in hearing and listening to what I think and say;
- I defend my assumptions and opinions without interest in others';
- I judge the other's opinions as wrong.

Associated with reflexion, is what Buber calls "semblance," or "seeming." Imagine a person's life that is dominated by "appearance," by how they look, by the image they present. Think of how you present yourself in conversation.

Buber writes of a friend, a master of conversation, who was sitting with another friend whom he describes as "a man of true conversation, but given more to objective fairness than to the play of the intellect, and a stranger to any controversy."

And then Buber surprises us with what can happen when "appearance," or one's own image refracts back and takes over the conversationalists. Buber writes:

> The friend whom I have called a master of conversation did not seek with his usual composure and strength, but he scintillated, he fought, he triumphed. The dialogue was destroyed.[5]

No matter how triumphant he might have felt, the *dialogue was destroyed*. It became, so quickly, so easily, a dialogue-destroying monologue—one person talking to him or herself.

Is it possible that qualities of monologue have become a national pastime? Remember, the basic movement of a life of "monologue" is not turning away from the other person but "reflexion," which is the withdrawal from accepting the other person in their particularity in favor of letting him/her exist only as one's own experience of them. Monologue stymies our cultural dialogue, deconstructs it, and frequently, and somewhat helplessly, curdles much of our interactions into a zero-sum game in

---

5. Buber, *The Knowledge of Man*, 88.

which: I win or you lose. Whatever happened to unreserved, face to face, authentic dialogue?

In Buber's little autobiographical book, *Meetings*, he portrays a time when he realized that his mother had been unable to practice turning toward him. In *Meetings* he writes:

> It cannot be a question here of recounting my personal life (I do not possess the kind of memory necessary for grasping great temporal continuities as such), but solely of rendering an account of some moments that my backward glance lets rise to the surface, moments that have exercised a decisive influence on the nature and direction of my thinking.[6]

In one such moment, Buber briefly describes the strange and sad story of his mother who left him when he was four years old. He later found out that she left to live with a Russian soldier. Buber was sent to live with his grandparents (on his father's side), and was raised largely by his grandmother Adele in Galicia, Austria. His grandparent's house had a large, rectangular inner courtyard surrounded by a wooden balcony on which one could circumnavigate the building. Here the four-year-old Buber once stood with an older neighbor girl who was responsible for watching him. They were leaning on the wooden railing:

> We both leaned on the railing. I cannot remember that I spoke of my mother to my older comrade. But I hear still how the big girl said to me: "No, she will never come back." I know that I remained silent, but also that I cherished no doubt of the truth of the spoken words. It remained fixed in me; from year to year it cleaved ever more to my heart, but after more than ten years I had begun to perceive it as something that concerned not only me, but all [humans].[7]

---

6. Buber, *Meetings*, 17. If Buber's most well-known work is his lyrical philosophical classic *I and Thou*, whose thesis is "all real living is meeting," his little book of autobiographical fragments, *Meetings* (1973), could be called a little classic, different in kind but equal in quality to *I and Thou*. That disclosure, the way he chooses to articulate himself, draws my attention all the more to the nature and direction of his thinking.

7. Ibid., 18.

Thirty years later, when Buber did meet his mother again, their encounter was racked with anxiety. Their distance, his abandonment and her alternative life, reinforced and kept a gulf between them.

Buber later coined the word "mismeeting" (*Vergegnung*) to designate the failure of real interactive mutuality between persons. As he indicated himself, much of what he learned about genuine meeting over the course of his life had its first origin in that hour on the balcony. His sense of genuine meeting, in other words, arose from his painful awareness of the ubiquity of mismeeting, of its universal effect on all humans. One thing that Buber's childhood experience of "mismeeting" taught him—which he only realized later—was that a sense of insecurity was often associated with meeting another person. Genuine meeting, Buber discovered, requires unconditional trust, a willingness to be vulnerable to the other.

What a strange conclusion. Through this experience of mismeeting, Buber first came to understand genuine meeting. Yes, it makes sense; Buber's use of the term "reflexion" (bending back on oneself) helps me understand why mismeeting occurs. When I am more interested in myself, in what I want, what I need, what I am doing, there is less than zero chance of really meeting another person. None.

Breaking Through Thinking

Recently, I was surprised to receive an untitled lyrical note from a longtime friend in North Philadelphia who has remained over the years a New York (his place of origin) sports fan. It contained a flyer announcing a poetry reading in which he was about to participate. His note read:

> Been doing a lot of thinking
> Asking questions, interviewing
> Reviewing the bidding
> Contemplating, gold plating
> Dynamics of that history
> Each part of the mystery
>
> It reveals as much as
> It covers
>
> Confusion, sorrow, sadness
> Anger release

A whole new perspective
And it's Mine to process

Both the philosopher Martin Buber and the physicist David Bohm would express concerns with this way of speaking about and understanding a "whole new perspective"—whether considering a whole person or a whole thing—through *thought*. For Buber, to grasp the whole of a person, it is necessary to relate to that person as a mutual presence, a *You* or *Thou*. Buber writes:

> If I face a human being as my Thou, . . . he is not a thing among things and does not consist of things . . . Thus human being is not a He or She, bounded from every other He or She, . . . but with no neighbor, and whole in himself, he is Thou and fills the heavens.[8]

But how is wholeness manifested? Is it really possible to become a "whole person"? It is not at all possible, according to Buber, if one thinks that by "whole," some action or set of actions must be performed to follow a definition of wholeness.

Because wholeness is actualized in genuine moments of engaging one another, the phrase *whole person* indicates a direction of movement, the presence of freedom in a healthy interplay between persons. This wholeness occurs on both sides of a genuine dialogue in each new situation with no other preparation than presence and readiness to respond.

The fundamental problem with thinking alone about wholeness according to David Bohm, is that there is no way thought can comprehend a person's wholeness—either another person or one's own self—because thinking is abstract, limited, defining. Bohm, rather, speaks of "participatory consciousness," of "participatory thinking." As for Buber, for Bohm genuine dialogue is a gateway to participatory thinking, a way to comprehend the whole meaning of who is doing the thinking, of what is being discussed.

Wholeness is not thinking, is not processing. Wholeness cannot be held onto, like an idea can. Wholeness is dialogical. Wholeness is participatory.

---

8. Martin Buber, *I and Thou*, 23.

Tuning In

Let's consider the reality of *turning* with some different terms. For me, Buber's use of the term *turning* makes perfectly good sense. Why? Because of the educative training I have received from a humanist, existential, psycho-sociological viewpoint. *Turning* refers to changing one's traction, one's state of being, one's direction of movement.

Yet it fascinates me that Alan Alda speaks like Buber without ever quoting or referring to Buber's writings. For example: the phenomenon of genuine, unreserved, mutually present dialogue cannot happen—is presumptuous and fallacious—unless prefaced by a mutual turning (both away from self and toward the other).

Alda, it seems, agrees. He was once invited to run a master class for actors. What made him eager to accept the invitation was his training in improvisational workshops, which he admits "changed me both as an actor and as a person."[9]

Improv, responding spontaneously to imagined situations or through an imagined persona to the situation before a person, helps him or her to make real contact with another. Communication, real communication, takes place because of real contact. And real contact takes place when one is able to focus on (to turn toward) the other. And that contact happened because his improv exercises enabled him to spontaneously focus all his attention on another person.

Here's how Alda described why he introduces actors to the value of practicing improvisation.

> At first, they stood looking at each other, just making up dialogue, as most everyone does to avoid being in the moment. When this happens, the words sound invented, unspontaneous—because when you're making up dialogue, you're thinking of what you'll say next; you're not focusing on the other person and reacting to them. I needed to get them to focus on something outside their own heads, so, coaching from the side, I asked them to use the imaginary environment, to make contact with the *place*.[10]

What's missing in this scene and when this scene replicates real life—what's most needed—is what Buber calls "turning," what Alda calls "tuned in."

9. Alda, *If I Understood You*, 9.

10. Ibid., 42.

There's no pretending in improvising. No *deciding* to behave differently. Instead, with our attention on the other person, and with a heightened ability to respond, we're tuned in to the present moment; we're in intimate contact with each other. It's as though the raw, vulnerable tissue of our most private self is in contact with the same vulnerable self of the other player.[11]

Usually called empathy, "tuning in" (to the other) is a perfectly harmonious chord to strike when discussing the necessity of "turning" to the other, in which we open up and become open to a spontaneous exchange of who we really are.

Yet here's a not overly dissimilar story, one in which what really stands out is the dialogical "spokenness of speech." Buber spent his first year of university studies in Vienna, the city of his birth and early childhood. It was the scholarly lectures at the university with its free discourse between students and teachers—the liberating exchange of questions and answers—that affected him more than anything else he had read in books. It was this dialogical interchange that disclosed the spirit of the "between" to him.

What most strongly affected him, however, was attending the Burgtheater, in its highest gallery. Often, he went there after lectures to watch dramatic performances. There Buber received the rightly spoken human word—the genuine spokenness of speech—into himself. Reflecting on this, Buber writes:

> Since then it has sometimes come to pass, in the midst of the casualness of the everyday, that while I was sitting in the garden of an inn in the countryside of Vienna, a conversation penetrated to me from a neighboring table (perhaps an argument over falling prices by two market wives taking a rest), in which I perceived the spokenness of speech, sound becoming 'Each-Other.'[12]

11. Ibid., 43.

12. Buber, *Meetings*, 31–32.

Meditation to Mutuality

Here, we come to one of the most difficult behavioral components of genuine dialogue, suspending (at least for an amount of time) the thoughts, feelings, reflections, generated by the egoic-I, by the self who I walk around thinking I am the person I call "me."

It is like when in the midst of what you are doing, like in the midst of writing this (which is happening now), my son-in-law walks in to my study area and, referring to a prior conversation says, "Kramer, are you ready?" I turn away from my desk (even though I'm on a roll, even though I'd rather continue writing in that moment, even though what I am writing about is 'turning' away from myself to greet the one who is addressing me), I turn.

There it is. The opportunity that includes a challenge, always a challenge, arrives at any moment, asking you that you stop, stop what you are doing and, as it were, start in a different direction, a different way, certainly with a different purpose.

All of us bring our assumptions into dialogue, according to David Bohm. What is called for is,

> to *suspend* those assumptions so that you neither carry them out nor suppress them. You don't believe them, nor do you disbelieve them; you don't judge them as good or bad. Normally, when you are angry, you start to react outwardly, and you may just say something nasty. Now, suppose I try to suspend that reaction. Not only will I now not insult that person outwardly, but I will suspend the insult that I make *inside* of me. Even if I don't insult somebody outwardly, I am insulting him inside. So I will suspend that, too. I hold it back, I reflect it back. You may also think of it as suspended in front of you, so that you can look at it—sort of reflected back as if you were in front of a mirror. In this way, I can see things that I wouldn't have seen if I had simply carried out that anger, or if I had suppressed it and said, 'I am not angry' or 'I shouldn't be angry.'[13]

It is important to note the difference between reflexion of the self back onto itself, and reflecting a thought or feeling of yourself back and holding it in front of you. In this way, you are not trying to suppress it, simply to suspend it. Now, you are called to be reframed, or redirected, or reoriented. Now, all of your attention is turned toward the other person, toward their concerns.

13. Bohm, *On Dialogue*, 22–23.

The act of "turning" (also called here "tuning-in," or later, "pivoting") is a phenomenological term. The Greek word *epoche* is a term that means putting aside judgments about non-evident matters. Herein lays the key. *Epoche* refers to a *practice*, not to an idea, not to an intellectual construct. *Epoche* points to an action-enabling action, to pausing and backing up that allows us a new kind of forward movement: open-minded, attentively present, deeply listening, and honestly responding.

Distractions, of course, are always there, associative thoughts and feelings forge their way into consciousness. As practitioners of meditation say, just observe the distractions without resisting them. Resistance will generate persistence. Let them pass through consciousness to clear one's attention for the other.

Once, while meditating silently along these lines in my parked car, for example, a remarkable event occurred. I had pulled over from a two-lane curving road into an unmarked parking area (where there was room for about a half a dozen cars) overlooking the Santa Cruz beach. Just down the beach a few hundred yards is the yacht harbor. From this pull-in space, beach-goers climb down onto the sand that, during the winter, provides space for more seagulls than swimmers. My meditation question that day was about mutuality. Where does the mutuality between myself and others occur?

On my dashboard I had placed a sheet of tablet paper on which I'd written a two-sentence description of mutuality as I experienced it in dialogue. After about fifteen minutes or so of closed-eyed listening into the silence, I heard the sound of someone walking on the gravel immediately outside of my car. Continuing to meditate with my eyes closed, suddenly I heard a woman's voice: "Are you alright? Do you need any help?"

Opening my eyes, I saw two young women standing outside my car looking in. "I'm fine," I said, rolling down my side window. The girl with short blonde hair and sunglasses said, "You weren't moving. We thought something might be wrong." The other, with shoulder-length brunette hair tied in pigtails, was equally concerned.

"That's because I was mediating," I said. "As it turns out, I'm in the midst of writing a book on dialogue. You could say," I smiled, "I'm here doing research." At that point, I extended my hand in a back and forth rotating motion to indicate that this very moment's interaction was an example of speaking dialogically. Of course, that was most likely a one-sided understanding.

Since they were somewhat interested in what I was saying, or perhaps intrigued by the energy with which I was saying it, they were in no hurry to move on. We fell into a dialogue. I learned that when they spotted me they were on their way to surf. Michelle (the brunette) was a student at the University of Hawaii in child psychology, and Donna was married and taught at a secondary level. We discussed their common interest in children, which interested me since one was married and one was single.

As they were about to leave, Donna noticed the piece of paper on my dashboard. "We thought that it might have been a note that you wrote for help."

"Do you want to read it?" I asked, looking at each of them. "You're married," I said to Donna, "why don't you read it. My question is 'Does it at all describe the mutuality you experience with your husband?'"

I handed her the page which was titled "Mutuality." She read: "a two-sided event in which the 'Passions and intentions of one person creatively compliment and enrich, even when contesting, the passions and intentions of the other. This intertwining interaction expresses itself in feelings of integrity, aliveness, belonging, and happiness.'" She paused, momentarily. "That's it" she said.

After the encounter, I was left with the sense that their response to my question was indeed manifested. I was amazed that two young women, whom I didn't know, would go out of their way, interrupting their plans, to make sure that I didn't need assistance and then that they would be willing to fall into conversation with me. I realized our mutuality through our relational energy between myself and these strangers was the spirit of mutuality.

The next day I saw Glen at the pool. He had come outside from the sauna/steam room area to see if I needed any assistance.

"I always need assistance," I joked.

"We help each other," he said.

"Speaking of that," I said, "yesterday something rather extraordinary happened in which the mutuality between myself and strangers became a little clearer. Each of us, in our unique way, experiences a bonding of spirit that united us, that joined us together in common concerns that we shared with each other."

"Thank you for that bouquet of words," he said, smiling with humility.

When we fully turn toward the other, but when the other doesn't fully turn toward us, mutuality does not happen. Martin Buber describes "mutuality" with evocative metaphors—a "memorable common fruitfulness," "an elemental togetherness," the "essential We," a "vital reciprocity," each generates and shapes each person's experience. While kindling feelings of completeness and integrity, without turning, the spirit that binds persons in mutuality cannot be fully present. Rather, these feelings arise from the mutuality between us, of trust, of caring, and of a willingness to enter into dialogues with an open mind. In this mutual presence, yet reaching out beyond either person, the innermost self of each person arises simultaneously.

Yet mutuality, which is necessary for genuine dialogue, does not occur simply by my intending it to occur. No matter how intensely I attempt to enter into genuine relationship with you, I cannot generate it myself. Neither can you. Like genuine dialogue, mutuality happens by virtue of relational turning, which arises from and generates the spirit of open-minded, open-hearted interactions.

Pivoting Around

Here's what it might look like if you discovered that what you most need to do to be fully ready for dialogue—to "pivot," around—from the fringes of yourself, from the places where you spend most of your time, the places where you use most of your energy, and pivot toward others who are waiting for your attention without your knowing it.

The pivot is unexpected as you have carved out a comfortable niche for yourself—making a comfortable living, enjoying the quality of your life, and railing (at least in your head) against those who think, look, act, conduct themselves differently from you.

Then one day you read a self-help book which gets your attention. It states that if any of the book's advice is to work, it must be prefaced by a complete "pivot," what Buber calls "turning," what Alan Alda calls "tuning in." In each case, it's as if one has to clear the deck, start fresh with a new focus. Now, full attention must be brought to the other—to their interests, to their concerns, to their questions.

A new world opens up: a world that capitalizes Relationships, interhuman Relationships. To begin with, you need no announcement, no image management. You are now responsible to other persons as well as to yourself.

By pivoting, you are able to write a new narrative about your life, to scratch out plan A, plan B, or plan C. In fact, scratch out your agenda; the agenda is the pivot itself.

Pivoting is not a performance art, nor a product of proficiency, nor is it a planned-out strategy. It is rather a deeply held ideal, or better put, a conviction that by pivoting one is able to become brand new *with* and *for* others.

When pivoting is mutual between persons engaging one another in the interhuman sphere, Buber calls its unfolding—the dialogical.

Metaphorically speaking, Buber characterized *mutuality* in relation to others as standing on the insecure "narrow ridge" between conflicting absolutes, between subjectivity and objectivity, right and wrong, between life and death itself. On this narrow ridge, where there is no certainty of expressible knowledge, a space opens where real mutuality between humans occurs. As I affect you, you affect me. Relationship is mutual. In its fullness, dialogue is mutually speaking and mutually listening.

To be authentic, dialogue must be *mutual*. For Buber, this mutuality does not mean simple unity or identity of the participants. Each person remains him or herself, remains uniquely different from others. Rather, direct, open, genuine dialogue connects men and women of different cultures and different beliefs. Real dialogue looks something like this:

1. **The mutuality of turning**, where each person in the relation turns away from self-interest and toward the other and tries to be as inquisitive, informative, and open-minded as possible.

2. **The mutuality of addressing**, where each person accepts the other person's right to be exactly who they are and affirms their right to believe as they do even if that belief is not shared.

3. **The mutuality of listening**, where each person tries to listen obediently, attentively, both to what is said and to what is beneath the surface of what is said.

4. **The mutuality of responding**, where each person tries to be clear, relevant, and pertinent to the discussion underway while trusting in the vital co-creative reciprocity and sacramental possibility of practicing genuine dialogue itself.

In one of his briefest definitions, Buber called authentic dialogue "Mutuality in speech."[14]

That is:

14. Martin Buber, *The Knowledge of Man*, 79.

When I stand in a common situation with the other and expose myself vitally to [their] share in the situation, as really [their] share. It is true that my basic attitude can remain unanswered and the true dialogue can die in seed. But if mutuality stirs, then the interhuman blooms into genuine dialogue.[15]

When, however, each participant does not have the other in mind, then in place of genuine dialogue we hear monologue disguised as dialogue. When there is no real mutuality of *turning, addressing, listening,* and *responding,* then no genuine dialogue can occur. Instead, pseudo-dialogue is prompted solely by the need for one to subjectively or objectively understand. Despite the warmest personal feelings associated with speaking, without mutuality in and through the discourse, monologue (speaking only to oneself) continues to disguise itself as dialogue. Speaking monologically, we have the illusion of getting beyond ourselves.

By contrast, and it's a huge contrast, Buber writes with lyrical definition:

Dialogue is fulfilled in its being between partners . . . who express themselves without reserve and are free of the desire for semblance, [therein] is brought into being memorable common fruitfulness which is to be found nowhere else. At such times, at each such time, the word arises in a substantial way between [persons] who have been seized in their depths and opened out by the dynamic of an elemental togetherness.[16]

Read this again: these words have the power to motivate you, to seize you in your depths, to open you out into the world. Instead of having dialogues, you mutually become a dialogue with others. You as we are spoken. You as we open out into the world, become a memorable mutuality found nowhere else.

Practicing Turning

Practicing turning engenders the dialogue process and enables your authentic existence to emerge. And here is what's most intriguing: the best teacher, the finest coach for learning the art of practicing turning is practice itself. No finer mentor exists than the very thing one wants to learn, that is by doing exactly what practicing needs you to do.

15. Ibid., 81.
16. Buber, *The Knowledge of Man,* 86.

Practicing turning is the direct expression of our human birthright, a way of engaging and being engaged—authentically—by others and, in the process, rediscovering who we really are. If I say to you, this practice has altered my life, it would be because, although I didn't always get what I wanted, by practicing turning, I certainly got what I needed. Rather than being a "silver bullet," fulfillment really comes from many places/actions that synergistically work together.

Practicing turning is as simple as catching yourself in the direction you are heading and then redirecting yourself toward the person in your presence. Like shifting into neutral, like pausing, like stopping and then re-starting yourself in another direction; the one thing necessary is to redirect your attention, your interest away from yourself (not always easy, I know) and toward the other person.

Of course, it will be necessary to try this maneuver a few times. But after you experience the mutuality of speaking and listening, which turning elicits, the process will become easier and easier.

So: stop, pause, shift your attention from yourself to the other and in the process give the other person the same attention you usually provide for yourself.

Here's a way to portray what practicing turning embodies:

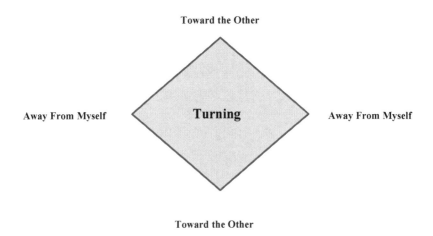

Turning Wholeheartedly

Away from Myself

- Away from self-affirming interests, narratives, assumptions, and thoughts
- Away from distractions, appearances, and impositions

Toward the Other

- By "temporarily suspending" one's own attitudes and beliefs
- By openly surrendering into relationships with the others (person, nature, animal, art, music . . .)

Buber speaks of a person's genuine turning toward the other, turning away from all self-preoccupations and distractions and toward full attention to the other. Everyone who turns in this way is turning toward another's specific, definitive, personal existence. It is only possible to make someone fully present by concentrating all your attention, all your energy, all your interests on how that person is listening to you and what that person has to say.

Turning is a very intimate interaction between specific persons who are ready to enter the process of dialogue. There it is! Try it. The other person is just waiting for you to bring yourself to them so that they can bring themselves to you.

2

Addressing

Back from Italy

"OH," SHE SAID, "I should mention that there was an Olympic-size pool available to visitors. But I had to deal with large mosquitoes at night by covering my entire body with a sheet up to here," she pointed underneath her nose, "It became a distraction."

"One larger than the mosquitoes, I'll bet," I added. "So much for my prayers that you would have a safe and *comfortable* trip," I laughed self-depreciatingly.

"Yes," she laughed along with me, "But the first part of the trip in Italy was extremely comfortable."

I hadn't seen my good friend Ziggy for more than six weeks, while she and her husband traveled to Italy—to Rome, to Venice, to Sicily. She then spent several weeks at a quasi-spiritual hermitage, quasi-artistic retreat. She is both a poet and a painter.

How, then, to greet her upon her return?

I bring this up because her return coincided with work on this section of the book. Since her attitude reflected our mutual sisterly/brotherly love for one another, I wanted to be aware of any clues she provided about what she wanted to talk about.

We each wanted to hear from the other.

What made Ziggy's return from Italy so wonderful after six weeks was that she was so open to listening and responding to others with spirit and animated speech.

Buber writes in its human manifestation, spirit animates the quality of our responses to others:

> Spirit is not in the "I," but between I and [the other]. It is not like the blood that circulates in you but like the air with which you

40

breathe. [You] live in the spirit if [you are] able to respond to [the other with your whole being].[1]

Ziggy and I also know and do our best to practice the solid give-and-take of speech-with-meaning. In these moments of deeply bonded relationship, we take our stand in mutually reciprocated speech. And this is why each of us continues to enter and reenter genuine dialogue with each other, and with others.

The central significance of lived speech is when, unlike dialectical exercises within the mind of a single thinker, speech becomes dialogically meaningful between persons. Why? Because we never know what we are going to say ahead of time, or how. We soon discover that our dialogical speech is ever-new, ever-creative because it occurs in consort with another's spirit, words, and life experience.

Most wonderfully, as Buber writes, the speech-with-meaning of genuine dialogue happens between us as we become a "genuine We."

> The genuine We is to be recognized in its objective existence, through the fact that in whatever of its parts it is regarded, an essential relation between person and person, between I and Thou, is always evident as actually or potentially existing. For the word always arises only between I and a Thou, and the element from which the We receives its life is speech, the communal speaking that begins in the midst of speaking to one another.[2]

For it is as We, ever-again as We that we speak meaningfully with others.

Accepting and Affirming

I was brimming with excited anticipation about what the visitors, years older now, would bring, would say, would laugh at, would reveal. It's hard to imagine any of the guests being timid—especially J. Benton White. Straight away in the interest of transparency I should tell you that over the last few days I have been swept away by realizing how much Benton helped me find my way home. And now, after eight years, he was coming to visit.

In the meantime while waiting, I survived, the new normal outrages we continued to live through, all the alert notifications, the distractions

1. Buber, *I and Thou*, 39.
2. Buber, *The Knowledge of Man*, 106.

meant to mis-inform us before the impossible possibility of the earth's outrage boiling over.

The visitors arrived full of a happy-to-see-me spirit: Professor Chris Jochim (former head of the Humanities Department, a specialist in Chinese Religious Traditions and Asian Studies) along with his wife, and Professor Benton White (former chair and founder of the Comparative Religious Studies Program at San Jose State University) along with his wife, entered the living room.

The visit was planned several weeks ago. Not that I had to prepare anything ahead of time, except to make sure that for such guests I had the best chai and the finest green tea available, along with my son-in-law's strong, freshly brewed Hawaiian coffee.

Off and on, at odd moments, I thought ahead to the visit. It was, after all, to be the first time in eight years that I would see Benton, the person who originally hired me and got my career going at San Jose State University. I often wonder, without that tenure track position and the benefits that trailed after it, where I would have wound up as a single parent of two daughters.

Benton's one act of hiring me had justified my leaving Philadelphia (with my then wife, my eight-month-old daughter, and no job) heading west in search of not only a new place to live, but a new teaching position (already becoming difficult to find). So more than anything, I wanted to express my gratitude *to* him and *for* him.

And now they were here. Always a proud, southern gentleman, Benton was walking with the help of a cane to assist him with balance. Now eighty-six, his bright smile led his careful steps, led him to the circular dining room table where he sensed (from the way the table was set up) we would sit. However, and surprisingly, he turned his chair halfway away from the table so he could both reach his coffee and at the same time direct his attention to my chair.

While the others were getting settled, once he was seated, I looked directly into Benton's smiling eyes and said: "Even though I've said this to you before, I will take to the grave my profound gratitude for your willingness to see through appearances and recognize the teacher beneath my less-than-professional look when we first met. You gave me an opportunity many would not have."

With gratitude, I took his hand and in the process felt his gratitude in return, felt the truth for him of a remark he once made: "Hiring you was the smartest thing I ever did."

A conversation ensued in which everyone felt acknowledged and affirmed. Beyond interesting, or popular, or political issues, we spoke of personal educative concerns in mutually supportive ways.

There was no pretense, there was gratefulness only. There were no behind-the-curtain judgments, there was respect only. There was no seeming, no pretending, there was vigilant honesty only. There was no selfishness, there was no reflexion, there was openness to each other only.

How was I to know that during the visit, after the morning rain was no longer coming down, I would hear Benton laugh deeply when I told of telling a medical assistant that I had a fine mind except in the medical field. And then, as he was about to leave, from his chair half turned away from the table, he would say to me, "I love you." My words fell short of what I felt. I said, "I love you, Benton."

Then after heartfelt hugs were exchanged, promises of future visits made, with Benton and his wife and Chris' wife already out the front door, Chris turned to me and said: "Ken, you are one of the few people I know—perhaps the only one—with whom shortly after visiting, I find myself in a deep conversation."

How powerful these words sounded coming from Chris, from Chris who is quiet, calm in a Buddhist sense, from Chris who rarely affirmed others.

I suppose it could be said that I was given a taste of my own "medicine," that is, the medicine of "affirmation." As Chris left, he gave me the interhuman gift of affirming a rarely noticed quality of my humanness. For a few minutes, I simply breathed in deeply. I could do no other.

After I wholeheartedly turn away from self-focus and give my complete attention to the person present before me, according to Buber another choice presents itself. How will I *address* the other? There are at least two meanings to the term addressing: first, it suggests the way we present ourselves to others (dismissive and judging or accepting and affirming); and second, it suggests the way we present ourselves to one another.

Hopefully it's clear by now that what distinguishes person-to-person relationships is "shared language." We present ourselves to others, and engage each other through speech. In the third Part of *I and Thou*, Buber continually returns to and focuses our attention on the significance of speech that occurs between persons:

> Only here does the primary word go backwards and forwards in the same form, the word of address and the word of response live in the one language, *I* and *Thou* take their stand not merely in relation, but also in the solid give-and-take of talk. The moments of relation are here, and only here, bound together by means of the element of the speech in which they are immersed.[3]

The basic formal expression of the interhuman realm, according to Buber, is "address and response." Speech without meaning and meaning without speech are equally inconceivable in this realm. In talking together, we build what Buber calls "speech-with-meaning." We enter personal relationships "through the solid give-and-take of talk."

"Here alone," Buber writes, "each person beholds and is beheld, recognizes and is recognized, loves and is loved." And most significantly, this type of relationship cannot be lost.

It is wonderful to spend part of an afternoon engaged in marvelous dialogue with a good friend with whom you'd have spent other afternoons (or mornings or evenings) in wonderful dialogue. The same can be said of course of a stranger. Nothing is assumed, there are no agendas.

We greet each other with a warm smile, deep breath, open spirit. We turn away distractions, be they listening to music or eating food, reading or writing. We turn completely and fully toward the other person.

I remember even now, after more than twenty years, meeting a complete stranger, a young woman who was a friend of one of my daughters and who wanted to discuss life at the university with an insider. I actually didn't want to be there at that moment because it would interrupt another project I was working on at home.

We met one afternoon in a downtown café and sat at their open-air tables where people were enjoying drinks and snacks.

3. Buber, *I and Thou*, 102–3.

Have you ever been in a similar situation? Not knowing this young woman, I *acceptingly* and *affirmingly* asked her: "So I'm interested in what brings you to your interest in the university at this time in your life?"

Sipping my coffee, I watched her facial expressions to catch any nuanced thoughts and feelings in her response. I recall saying, "Don't forget to find out this . . . ," and "Make sure that you have asked about that . . ."; but I was also able to add a personal touch, "When I was in your situation, I wish I would have known about . . . ," and "I wish someone would have told me what to do when . . ."

The deeper her interests grew, the greater my attention grew; the greater my attention grew, the deeper her listening became, the more imaginative her questions were.

Time and space seemed to vanish: she was there; I was there; We were there.

What we didn't know of each other no longer seemed to matter; no, we knew each other in and through our dialogue. In and through our dialogue, we were discovering a togetherness, unlike others. Here each speaker and each listener became mutually stimulated, mutually robust.

Instead of having, or participating in a dialogue, we *became* a dialogue. We were not separate from our speech, we were not using words. In those moments of genuine dialogue our strangeness morphed into a genuine We-ness.

Addressing the other brings with it a wonderful interconnected, two-sided meaning. On one hand, it means "facing"; the other, presenting yourself, approaching the other: What's your attitude? What are your gestures, your body's positioning? Is it totally open and welcoming? Or is it partially cautious, and restrictive? Do you hold yourself back? Are you uncertain, insecure?

What is needed, if dialogue is to be genuine—and it's not impossibly difficult—is trusting in the reciprocity of the process. Each of the partners, that is, has to lean into the mutuality of exchange. Without resistance due to physical appearance, to social position, due to religious beliefs, due to sexual orientation, due to age, education, job, political views, one steps into an encounter. "All real living is meeting."

As we have seen, the word *addressing* also refers to *speaking* (whether with words or with glances and gestures, or even silence). Speaking is a communication tool that enables us to present ourselves diligently and honestly, openly and listeningly.

Real dialogue does not mean chatter, nor judgmental associations nor partial speech in which full honesty is withheld, it means rather, "speech-with-meaning."[4]

Speaking meaningfully withholds nothing, is not judgmental, yet is not without points of view, and is fully open to the other's response. Meaningfully speaking flows over language with reliable, trustworthy words that characterize who you really are, not just who you seem to be or want to be seen as being.

Real meeting takes place when each person *accepts* the other as a wholly unique person and *affirms* the other's views and beliefs even though they differ from yours. However, it is not an inner experience. Buber writes: "Rather, in that moment something happens in the [person]. At times it is like a light breath, at times like a wrestling bout, but always it happens."[5]

Rather than an inner experience, the twofold communication prefaces an event, a meeting that occurs between and among people, genuine dialogue happens.

Upon meeting another person, no matter who that person is, according to Buber, a spontaneous ritual of *acceptance* and *affirmation* occurs, a ritual greeting that weaves two attitudes, two basic stances together.

Actually the word just used, "attitude," can be misleading if read as a psychological reaction to reality; it might be better to speak of acceptance and affirmation as a twofold communication of your basic stand.

Speaking Ever-New

It doesn't take long to recognize that in our shared living environment—the cosmos—we all share with one another differently. In a similar fashion, our fundamental tool for communicating—speaking—is practiced differently. That is, the manner, rhythm, and pace with which we transfer meaning back and forth between ourselves is uniquely expressed.

When Buber spoke meaningfully, he was not referring to the qualitative measureable content of our words, rather—and this is the

4. Buber, *The Knowledge of Man*, 107.
5. Buber, *I and Thou*, 109.

eye-opening "rather"—he pointed to the qualitative presence of our speaking. Whatever else it represents, speaking in response to another's speaking portrays our ever-new birthright—freely given yet needing to be developed—expressing itself.

Real dialogue, for Buber, came to be the ground of all that is true and creative between people. This came to be the place where every day in every moment mystic interactions occurred.

Skye was late, so I continued working on this section of the manuscript. When he arrived, he sat in the computer chair to the side of my desk and removed his jacket. I offered him—which he accepted—a cup of freshly made organic coffee, the kind that relaxes you into being picked up. Skye, after losing a friendly dog, after retiring from his job at University of California, Santa Cruz, and then going through a divorce with his wife (all in several months), had fallen into a dark depression. His circumstances had been unkind.

"I've been listening to some of Alan Watts' CDs on spirituality," he says. "According to Watts, when you are stuck in a rut, when you are no longer certain where to stand, where to go, or what to say, then it is helpful to step back and *watch*. Watch what others around you are doing." And then, pausing, he added, "I'd like to hear what you would say about this?"

First, *this* and then *that* flashed through my consciousness, "Two things," I said: "The second first. Second, I suggest that you search YouTube for a dialogue between Professor Maurice Friedman and Alan Watts titled, 'Beat Zen, Beat Hasidism.'

"Friedman was my teacher at Temple University back in the 60s. In fact, his book, *My Dialogue with Hasidism: Hallowing the Everyday*, opened my attention to Buber's spirituality, especially the deep similarly between Hasidic and Zen mysticisms.

"The first thing is about why, being influenced by Buber's Hasidism as I am, I would modify Watts' view. Temporarily stepping back and watching can be an excellent first step as long as you don't get stuck watching. Doesn't Watts often say that we need to be aware of living in the present, right here and right now?"

"Yes," Skye agreed. "So, the future doesn't even exist!"

"Then, if this very moment, this present moment is all there is, and you decided because of feeling stuck spiritually, to sit back and watch, you and I would remain silently watching each other, right!"

Skye reluctantly agreed, taking a swig of his coffee. "For me," I said, "When I am the stand that I take, I am a dialogical person. Whenever I meet another (such as you) in a common situation (such as this) and receive a question specifically addressed to me, I feel called to personally respond unreservedly, to answer your question at least with the intense honesty with which it was asked."

"Silently watching the other would be, therefore, a cop-out, a refusal to be human."

What I said flowed forth without interpretation. "By the way," I added, "the beauty of practicing a dialogical stand is that your response is all we know, even when your response is to the same question that you've been asked before. It is new because you are always new, the situation is always new, and the language used is always becoming new."

Where dialogue genuinely exists, it is always new. Brand new. Dialogical speech, of course, depends on what I have to say and what it elicits from others, and vice versa. From Buber's perspective, I must be intent "to raise into an inner word and then into a spoken word what I have to say at this moment, but *do not yet possess as speech*."[6]

When Skye and I began our conversation, I had no idea what I was going to say, except that it would be honest, present, and attentive. But before realizing it, I heard myself referring to another Alan Watts teaching about the eternal now, about always being in the present.

In the context, it felt natural to apply the necessity of speaking to the other: of asking questions, of thinking aloud, along with the other, of expressing my life-stand in response to Watts' suggestion about "watching." One is called by the cosmos to respond, especially when someone comes to seek your council, your advice, your viewpoint.

We come here to one of those times, when Buber writes a dramatically appropriate paragraph:

> Where the dialogical word genuinely exists, it must be given its right by keeping nothing back . . . Everything depends on the legitimacy of 'what I have to say'. And of course, I must also be intent to raise into an inner word and then into a spoken word what I have to say at this moment, but do not yet possess as speech. To speak is both nature and work, something that grows and something that

---

6. Buber, *Knowledge of Man*, 80, italics mine.

is made, and where it appears dialogically in the climate of great faithfulness, it has to fulfill ever anew the unity of the two.[7]

However, what has been said? There are times when understanding what Buber is saying requires re-reading and re-reading his words. At times, in these movements—and this is one of them—I re-read Buber's words in their reverse order, from bottom to top.

To fulfill the ever-new unity of nature and work, in a climate of great trust, is to speak of both nature (instinct) and work (learning). Something that grows and something that is made are unified in dialogue.

In a moment when I do not yet possess speech for what really needs to be said, I must be intent on raising to legitimacy what I have to say.

Everything depends on the legitimacy of what I have to say, first from an inner word and then into a spoken word.

Fittingly, just before he died, Maurice Friedman finished his final and most intimate book on Buber titled, *My Friendship with Martin Buber* (2013). Springing from Friedman's relationship with Buber, beginning in the summer of 1950 and ending with Buber's death in 1965, this work takes us from Friedman's earliest contact with Buber, through Buber's three visits to America, his wife's death, and Friedman's four-month stay in Jerusalem. To trace this chronology, Friedman draws extensively from his personal collection of letters between Buber and himself.

In the book's opening paragraph, Friedman speaks of a decisive quality that he inherited from Buber, "of deeply caring about responding to one's unique personal call with a wholeness of the being that includes genuine decision and what the Hasidim called *kavana*—deep inner intention."[8]

The book's Epilogue contains Friedman's "Memorial Address" given at the Martin Buber Memorial Meeting, Park Avenue Synagogue, July 13, 1965. Commenting on the difference between a charismatic *zaddik* master and Buber's wrestling again and again with his faith, Friedman remarks that "Buber's existence was 'continually renewed decision' [or continually renewed dialogue]—from his readiness to meet whoever came to see him to his refusal to deal with unreal questions."[9]

7. Ibid., 86.

8. Friedman, *My Friendship with Martin Buber*, 1.

9. Ibid., 161.

Friedman continues that, in the dialogue between Buber and American psychologist Carl Rogers, which took place at the University of Michigan in 1957, Buber announced what Friedman calls his most precious gift to all persons of our age: "Trust, trust in the world because this human being exists."[10]

Again, this is one of those moments when my teacher's teacher becomes mine, when Buber's words become mine, when Buber's "trust in the world" becomes mine because *you* exist, or as Brother David Steindl-Rast calls his memoir, which he wrote at ninety years old, *I Am Because of You.*[11]

Again, Buber's words about how glorious "growing old" can be when a person does not unlearn how to begin, have become mine.

Buber tells a poignant story of meeting a noble old thinker at an academic conference where he gave a lecture on folk traditions. Buber was happily surprised to hear the man with steel-gray locks ask participants at the beginning of his talk "to forget all that we believed we knew about his philosophy . . ." As a result of the First World War, which brought reality so close to the noble thinker, he began thinking in a new way. The thinker taught Buber (and me along the way of writing this):

> To be old is a glorious thing when one has not unlearned what
> it means to *begin;* this old man had even perhaps first learned it
> thoroughly in old age. He was not at all young, but he was old in a
> young way, knowing how to begin.[12]

The Orange-Haired Mortician

Terina, an orange-haired single mom, who is studying to be a mortician, has a sixteen-year-old daughter. We had often talked by the ocean about her desire to live on a boat, to sail around different continents in her life-long quest for the Terina fish, which would bring her desires to fruition. Recently, Terina told me a very powerful story with powerful consequences.

Despite more than forty years difference in our ages, and differences in upbringing and culture, we continue to get along famously. On the one hand, Terina knew a lot about the ocean and the changes in temperature, in fish breeding, and fears she had about the extinction of species. On the

10. Ibid.

11. Brother David Steindl-Rast, *I Am Because of You.*

12. Buber, *Meetings*, 49.

other hand, I was extremely curious about ocean life since I had been living near the ocean (both Atlantic and Pacific) for all of my life. This is not to mention that each of us willingly and carefully listened to the other and spoke to the heart of each other.

"No," I would caution her each time she talked about seeing a boat she liked that was for sale, remembering the days when I practiced selling real estate, recalling the numerous stories I heard about no-time boat owners buying a boat to live on, only to realize they couldn't continue living in such a small space.

"Don't do it," I would say to her proposals to buy a boat. "You may regret it." On her side of the conversation, Terina was thinking and often said, "I'm gonna do it anyway, you'll see."

But this was not all we talked about. We talked about raising children; we talked about books and movies that had deeply impressed us; and we talked about music, lots and lots of music. Last of all, although first of all in my ranking of importance, we talked about talking, about the magical grace of dialogue.

At least once during our conversations, usually toward the end of them, we talked briefly about dialogue, its purpose, practice, and its poignancy.

Actually, however, this is a mother-daughter story. I have known Terina's daughter for as long as I've known her, about four years. She began babysitting my grandchildren (I live in the same house with my daughter, her husband, and their children) a few years ago. It was from that time forward, I had been emphasizing in my conversations with Terina the need for her to develop a dialogical relationship with her daughter, Lilly.

And then this. It had been more than a year since I had seen her last. Now sixteen, while learning how to drive, Lilly had been having a string of dreams about being driven by a teenage friend (illegal in the state of California) and winding up tied to the car's roof when the friend drove it accidentally off the wharf and into the bay. Each time, she awakened before dying.

Having discussed dreams with Terina before, and having given her a book I had written, *Death Dreams*, Terina asked me, "So, what's your interpretation of this dream?"

"It's really two dreams," I said, "which reinforce two things, each of them are good for Lilly. First, she is clearly not yet ready to drive by herself; and second, she knows that it is dangerous to be driven around by another teenager." But that's not the story here. The story is far more interesting. Indeed, the story indirectly takes me at least back to my earlier conversations with Terina.

And here's why. When Terina told me what had recently occurred between her and her daughter, I was surprised and had a large smile across my face. I say that because things were sometimes rather strange between them. Lilly was not unlike many teenagers who think and feel and act as if they, and only they, know what's best to do in all situations.

Here's what Terina said: "The other day, actually about a month ago, I went into Lilly's room to check on her pet bird. There, I easily discovered, I say easily because it wasn't hidden, a tiny tin on her dresser. Usually I give her total trust and privacy and don't go into her room and mess with her things, but this tin got my attention and my curiosity. So I decided to open it. Inside the tin there were three half-burned cigarettes. I was furious, I wanted to call her out and scold her for this extremely bad choice. However, suddenly, I remembered when I was her age, doing the same thing. Regardless of my mom's adamant demands for me to quit, I continued smoking. I smoked until I figured out on my own that it was not a good habit.

"I decided rather than approaching her with anger and disappointment, to simply leave a little note in her tin stating: 'Let's talk, love Mom.'"

And here we come to what I consider the most fascinating element in this story—Lilly's response. At least her daughter's response through Terina's perspective. This, to the best of my memory, is word-for-word what Terina told me about what Lilly did. Terina said:

> Finally, after a month or so of anticipation, Lilly came forth and one day said to me, "I got your note." That was all I needed to hear, because that said to me that she was ready to talk. I immediately reassured her that smoking is *not* OK; it is unhealthy; it is illegal to smoke. But I understand the motivation for it. I then let her know I am on board to help her quit, and if she feels addicted to cigarettes, we together can conquer it with support groups, lifestyle changes, and nicotine gum.
>
> Lilly's response was wonderful. She reassured me she isn't smoking regularly, but occasionally does smoke socially with friends. She is pretty sure she is not addicted. She then immediately thanked me for not flying off the handle and punishing her. She thanked me for giving her the power to discuss the issue with her on her own terms, like an adult.

When I heard this, a smile spread across my face. Why? Because of Terina's reaction, which is at the heart of dialogue—namely, to: 1) accept her daughter as a unique person who has the same right to speak and be heard as she does; and 2) affirm her daughter's right to express her views even if they disagree with Terina's.

"A Great Man," T. S. Eliot Said

It was an early summer London day. Men in wool suits smoked cigarettes on the way to and in their offices. And while he didn't know how special it would be, T. S. Eliot was about to meet the Jewish-German existential philosopher of dialogue, Martin Buber, before Buber left London on his first trip to America.

Their meeting had been arranged by Ronald Gregor Smith, who translated several of Buber's books, including Buber's lyrical classic, *I and Thou*, which Eliot, as an avid student of philosophical texts, had read and appreciated. It may even have been that Eliot re-read parts of the well-known text to refresh his memory before the meeting.

Buber and Eliot were brought together, along with J. H. Oldham and Melville Chaning-Pearce. The main topic of their conversation was based on a book that Buber had just finished, *Two Types of Faith*, about the Jewishness of Jesus and the inaccessibility of understanding Jesus in simple, third-person statements. It is worth noting that for Eliot, Buber's *I and Thou*, which Eliot read in English, had a profound effect on modern religious thought. Although Eliot was very shy, he was nevertheless, directly frank, which, as Maurice Friedman notes, "Buber did not usually find with persons when they first met him." Of his meeting with Buber, Eliot wrote to Friedman:

> I once had a conversation with Dr. Buber . . . and I got the strong impression that I was in the company of a great man. There are only a very few men of those whom I have met in my lifetime, whose presence has given me that feeling.[13]

When Buber told Friedman about his meeting with Eliot, five days after it took place, Friedman asked Buber: "Don't you find that your opinions and those of T. S. Eliot differ in important respects?" Buber responded, "When I meet a man I am not concerned with his opinions but with the man."[14]

---

13. Friedman, *Encounter on the Narrow Ridge*, 334, 419.

14. In 1962, five years before Buber died, Eliot joined other prominent signatories in supporting the nomination of Martin Buber for a Nobel Prize in literature.

That response, more than any other as I have indicated in the "Introduction," invited me all the more to meet—really meet—my teacher's teacher.

Friedman was referring to Eliot's poetry, which some critics had called anti-Semitic. Buber's response to first meeting Eliot was that he, Buber, did not meet an opinion, but met a person. Buber was able to bracket others' opinions of Eliot so that he could have a real encounter.

Friedman would later say that his first meeting with Buber was nothing less than an invitation into a new world, a world that called him to confront his own limitations and to explore new horizons.

Buber's penetrating gaze into Friedman's eyes placed a demand on Friedman to suspend his opinions about Eliot, in order instead to *meet* him as a human being. Incredible! It was *that* distinction (between meeting your opinions of a person and meeting the real person) which opened my mind's eyes.

I asked myself: "What if the most important person is always the person you are with, the one you are addressing, and the one who is addressing you?" This is, at least from Buber's view, the always-changing, most important person in your life, the one who is here right now. And I knew that Buber's answer to the rhetorical question had become my answer as well.

"There Are no Great Men," Buber Said

We are fortunate here to have a rare inside glimpse of Buber in his Jerusalem home, where he lived from 1938 until he died in 1965. As you read through this vignette, pay special attention to the way Buber welcomed, addressed, and affirmed complete strangers brought into his study. In a letter to me, Phyllis Anderson, a visiting student, wrote:

> In 1963 I had a grant to study in Israel for six weeks. I traveled there with a group directed by Professor Menahem Mansoor—at that time head of the Department of Hebrew and Semitic Studies, University of Wisconsin, Madison.
>
> Dr. Mansoor was well known in Israel and we were invited to have tea and a short meeting with Martin Buber at his home in Jerusalem.
>
> It was hot but the stone house had tiled floors, high ceilings, and window blinds that let the breeze through, but moderated the sunlight. Every room was lined, ceiling to floor with books and large library ladders on rollers, even the dining room. There was a very young child playing with a kitty. After tea we stood around the

dining room and in came a frail, fragile looking old man in house shoes. The child crawled into his lap and he spoke briefly, then told us we could ask questions. We were all awed by the situation but there were questions. Finally, he indicated that he was tired, so only one more question. Someone asked, "Dr. Buber who do you think has been the greatest man in history?"

Buber paused a moment, almost as if surprised and said quietly: "Why, there are *no* great men, only useful ones." Then he rose, smiled a gentle smile, bowed slightly, and shuffled out to the kitchen where women were preparing a meal. Our group exited in total silence.[15]

The phrase "great men" can be used categorically in a way that reduces a person's uniqueness to a one-sided, formulaic catchword. Rather than "great" persons, Buber was more interested in meeting "useful" persons, persons who are capable of whole-heartedly responding to the unique particularities of the other. It is, therefore, somewhat counter-productive to try painting Buber heroically. Instead, we are more concerned with Buber's usefulness, the immediate applicability of his life's work to our ways of living and knowing. The "life of dialogue" is lived, not emulated. And, as we are seeing, it is grounded in the uniqueness of each person.

Entering into dialogical relationships represents a high peak of relational life, a sudden flash that illumines a person's way. When two (or more) persons simultaneously step into direct relationship, a new quality of communication springs forth.

It would be as if each person had a not-so-secret secret passion for drawing caricatures and cartoons. The new quality of communication opens a co-authored comic strip in which this new quality finds itself renewed and released within the authenticity of their dialogue.

Making (The Other) Present

Encountering the presence of another person is not, as one might at first think, just awakening one's perceiving senses to recognize the other's physical presence. No, more is necessary. The completion of making the other present involves imagining, as well, the specific person as a whole and unique being. In such a way, we perceive the other as a dialogical partner to whom we willingly listen and responsibly respond.

15. Phyllis Anderson originally sent this vignette in a letter to the author.

Underlying both *accepting* and *affirming* the other, whether friend or stranger, is the single most important component of dialogue—mutual presence. Buber points to the necessity of making the other person present through imagining to yourself what another person is at this very moment wishing, feeling, perceiving, and thinking.

Beyond that, Buber means practicing the ability to imagine/realize the other person's potential wholeness. Buber writes:

> To 'mean' someone in this connection is at the same time to exer-
> cise that degree of making present which is possible to the speaker
> at that moment. The experiencing senses and the imagining of the
> real which completes the findings of the senses work together to
> make the other present as a whole and as a unique being, as the
> person that he is. But the speaker does not merely perceive the one
> who is present to him in this way; he receives him as his partner,
> and that means that he confirms this other being, so far as it is for
> him to confirm.[16]

Making another person present involves both: 1) acceptance of a person in this moment, and 2) acceptance and affirmation of the person's potential.

By making the other present, we confirm the inmost self-becoming of our partners in dialogue. In this perspective, Buber distinguished three interrelated orientations: *acceptance, affirmation,* and *confirmation*. These inter-linked behaviors move from generic acceptance (accepting the other as a person like ourselves), to specific affirmation (affirming the other in their unique historic, cultural, or ethnic personhood), and confirming the other (validating the other's present stance and their direction of move-ment into the future).

Confirmation, furthermore, adds to acceptance and affirmation the willingness to continue challenging the other to move in the direction their life is taking. I affirm the other's will as well as their identity. Since these three behaviors are integral for implementing an effective practice of dia-logue, it is essential to grasp their interconnections.

While teaching at San Jose State University in the 1990s, as a part of a "Death, Dying, and Religions" class, I conducted a series of interviews with Death professionals like Kübler-Ross before the class in an auditorium set-ting. I began each interview with a version of the question: "What's missing

16. Buber, *The Knowledge of Man*, 85.

from the way in which most of us think/feel about death/dying, the presence of which would liberate us from our fears?"

I felt at the time that this question would offer each professional an opportunity to open up with their special approach to the subject. While I prepared for each interview by reviewing the work/writings of each interviewee, I deliberately did not write out preplanned questions. Instead, I wanted the dialogue to flow spontaneously from each person's initial response. This practice felt to me most real, most honest.

But here let me go back to the beginning of each interview. I had never met any of the interviewees beforehand. Usually, they arrived 10–15 minutes before class, except Ram Dass (Richard Alpert), who arrived after class had already started. I can still see him smiling, striding down a side aisle from the back of the auditorium. I had to introduce myself to him and to the class at the same time. Fortunately his sense of humor made it easy.

Now to the point. Prior to conducting this series of interviews, I went to San Francisco to interview a well-known radio interviewer on the art of conducting interviews with politicians, musicians, actors, and entertainers. Because he was an accomplished interviewer, I wanted to ask him about his artistry, his techniques. I was particularly curious about his opening address.

We sat across from one another at a rectangular table. A microphone sat on the table between us. At one point, I looked directly into his eyes and asked, "What's the most important thing about interviewing someone?" He gazed back into my eyes and said, "Most importantly, the person you are interviewing must feel comfortable, feel relaxed."

That's where the discussion of the second element to genuine dialogue should begin. That is, after *turning away from* self-preoccupations and *toward* the otherness of the other, we then are confronted with *addressing* the other(s) before us.

It seems to me that the San Francisco interview was spot on—we need to make others comfortable, accepted, whether stranger or friend, and relay one more easily into a conversation when they (and you) feel relaxed. Assuming this, Buber's principles provide us more direction.

Addressing Students

The conditions couldn't have been more ideal. Early September, North Carolina; a small private college set on blue-green acres in a sleepy little city forty-five minutes from Chapel Hill; less than a thousand respectful, well-mannered Southerners riding the maturity train on their parents' dime under manicured-trees. I was not worried about the number of students who would show up. I had played basketball before crowds of ten thousand fans; I had preached before several hundred congregants at once; in seminary, I had sung in a folk trio music like Peter, Paul and Mary's "If I Had a Hammer" to Pete Seager's "We Shall Overcome" in high school school auditoriums.

It wasn't being in front of many students that prompted my nervousness. It was not knowing what questions they might ask. It was the possibility of not knowing how to answer a specific question. Would my teaching authority crumble if I was caught without an answer?

Into a "Modern British and American Poetry" class of twenty-five freshman and sophomores I walked, decked out in a sports jacket and tie and carrying pages and pages of newly typed notes and books of poetry littered with markings. After setting my materials on the front desk, I looked up to make eye-contact, stranger-to-stranger, with the students.

Smilingly, as the new teacher on the block, I removed my sports jacket to present myself more informally. Then, looking at the students (as if there should be no dead air), I uttered: "Phewph!" (with a slightly over-exaggerated expression of relief). "Ahh, that's much better." Laughter followed.

The unintended dramatic playfulness of that first pre-teaching gesture in that small southern college classroom awakened something buried in me. I followed that laughter with a spontaneous first question: "Any questions?" This time the laughter was a little louder, a little longer.

Feeling much more relaxed and at home, I told them who I was, where I had studied, and why I was so interested in the course material.

"Ohh," interrupting myself, "wait a minute! I forgot what's really important here." Pause. "Moi," I said, "Me!"

More laughter.

Instinctively, while they were focused on the humor in the situation, I segued into announcing the class content, required readings, grading, and office hours.

I began to feel more emboldened and dropped any pretense that I was anyone other than, simply, myself.

Thus it began—my first laughter-infused class presentation. While it took years to hone the performance art I had stumbled into at that first class, I walked away elevated, realizing how natural the dialogic process of teaching (talking, listening, questioning, and responding) was for me. And the more laughter, the better.

Now, more than forty years later as a retired professor and published author, when I am given the opportunity to speak to a group of students, I take the invitation very seriously. I especially want to know as much as I can about the audience in order to make them present by thinking, feeling, and experiencing as I imagine them to think, feel, and experience.

I realize, moreover, how significant it is for me to "read the room" for signs and signals of address. For questions and interests which will be brought forward.

And then I prepare to begin as if unprepared, as if "starting out where we left off," all the while realizing the subject matter, talking about how we are a dialogue, really needs to be practiced rather than talked about.

To make a responsible response, one that properly situates the material, a person holds their ground, which allows them to make an honest and sober response from the beginning. You don't remove yourself into another realm. You stand in the place where you are subject to similar effects as the others. In other words, you persevere in the specific concrete circumstance at hand, not trying to avoid it.

If I don't respond from where I am standing, my words aren't worth much. Holding one's stand in the world, as it is given to us, presents us with methods to express ourselves honestly in each situation in such a way, each of the dialogic partners, and the dialogue itself, can be genuine.

And it's not difficult in that, like addressing anyone, no matter how they look, or how they hold (or don't hold) themselves, or what beliefs/opinions persuade them, it is always necessary to take into account their potential, their direction of movement in and through life. As with a room full of new students, remaining open, to another's potential development into who they are becoming does not mean trying to shape that potential in ways commensurate with your beliefs or with what you think would be appropriate.

Rather, addressing suggests a questioning support, a challenging discernment of who and where they stand. Just as one (I/you) take a dialogical stand—present ourselves dialogically—when we meet others (whether for the first time, or the tenth time), it is vitally important to remain open not only to the presence of the other but, as well, their (and our) future.

Interpersonal creativity is called for to pick up signals, signs, and silences that suggest certain questions to discuss, certain possibilities to consider. We are all always becoming new.

Practicing Addressing

It should be mentioned that practicing addressing is made easier by turning. Once you are in the presence of, paying attention to, focusing on another person, then, and only then are you ready to, and is the other ready to receive your accepting affirmation.

Just like you, this person comes from a family with a living history; just like you, this person fears the unknown, suffers painful experiences, seeks connection with others, and tries to keep his or her mind and heart open. Just like you, this person flails and fails, struggles and succeeds, hates and loves. This person who is right here is just like you.

Do you ever, even for a minute, think about how wonderful your life is, how wonderful it is to be alive, rejoicingly alive? Doing this, I suggest forms a perfect prelude for practicing addressing. How? Simply this: by inviting the feelings of gratitude that come with recognizing the unique gift your life is, the more gratitude flows through you, the more it becomes natural to extend your meetings with acceptance, your greetings with affirmation for and to the other person. I'm suggesting that expressing personal gratitude leads naturally to interpersonal acceptance.

Here's a way to portray it:

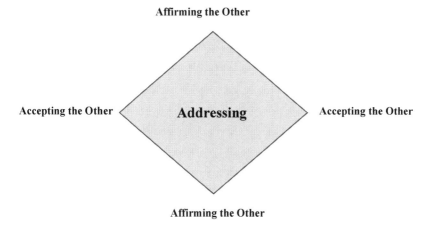

Addressing Attentively

Accepting the Other

- No matter their political, religious, ethical, cultural beliefs, just like me
- The other's presence regardless of race, culture, gender, sexual preference

Affirming the Other

- As a unique person who has the same right to speak and be heard as you do
- The other's right to express beliefs and viewpoints even when different from yours

Buber speaks of a person genuinely addressing the other, turning away from all self-preoccupations and distractions and toward full attention to the other. Everyone who addresses others in this way, addresses their specific, definitive, personal existence. It is only possible to make someone fully present by concentrating all your attention, all your energy, all your interests upon how that person is able to listen to you and what that person has to say.

It has been said before and will be said again that in order to address the other fully, it is necessary to become aware not only of what the other says "through our senses," but what they are thinking and feeling and experiencing at that moment. Addressing is not just a part of human nature, a part of social ritual, a part of family rites of passage, but is a very intimate interaction between specific persons who willingly trust the process of dialogue.

PART II

Interactions

3

Listening

Sun-Filled Voices

It was a sun-filled, cloudless blue sky day when a friend brought a friend to my open study. We began talking. I was ready to listen. This morning I had been introduced to a young, newly married, dark haired woman from Brazil. Carolina was full of thirty-year-old energy, full of being-in-a-new-culture, in a new relationship, and full of curiosity and conversation.

We easily slid into a back-and-forth exchange in which I asked her: "So what first attracted you to your husband?" This question, as she began to think about it, was then followed by another. "And what continues to attract you to him, now that you have been married a half year?" And so it went.

During the ensuing conversation, she pointed to a book lying alone on the corner of my desk near the microwave on the bookshelf where I warm my coffee while writing, as I just had.

"Are you reading this book?" she asked carefully looking at Martin Buber's face drawn on the cover of Maurice Friedman's book *Martin Buber and the Eternal*.

"Oh," I said, smiling, "that's a book about my teacher's teacher. It is written by my teacher, Maurice Friedman, about his teacher, Martin Buber, who has now become my main teacher."

"Umm . . . , what do you mean?" she murmured while continuing to ponder the jacket design of Buber's right hand against his right cheek and the right side of his forehead.

"I mean to call attention to Buber's teaching of genuine dialogue, which I first learned through Buber's student, Maurice Friedman, my major teacher at university. Let me put it this way—my teacher's teacher has now become my life-time teacher," I replied.

She smiled as if she not only understood, but as if she may have had a similar experience. "Now that I have retired from teaching, I spend a lot of time writing," I said. Seeing my large desk, the top of which is filled with books, it was easy for her to hear me say, "I'm a writer. It's my passion. It's what I wake up to do. It's what I fall asleep thinking of: ideas, possibilities, stories, moments from Buber's life. Always thinking . . ."

"What are you writing now?" Carolina asked. Her dark hair was pulled into a bun at the back of her head, accentuating her ivory teeth-filled smile that at any moment seemed ready to break open into a conversation in which a new world would be revealed.

Each time someone asks me this question—"What are you writing?"— I need to assess the context: what has led the person to ask such a question; how serious is the questioner; how deeply can I go into the details?

I realized that since we had just met each other, this was not the right time to be longwinded. I began, "It's a brief book on dialogue, on Buber's dialogue, which comes after years of studying the dialogical philosophy of Martin Buber, along with years of my own practice. The book describes Buber's dialogical practice. It arranges and portrays dialogue's four stages (*turning*, *addressing*, *listening*, and *responding*). When practiced, they enable us to discover who we really are."

Before I could say anymore, I noticed that she had shifted her attention to our French Bulldog as it ran into the room suggesting that another event was about to happen. So I stopped talking about the book. Ok, but what would I have said next? What would be the most important follow-up to make?

Of course, the most important next thing to say completely depends on the listener, on how the listener responds to her first hearing of the four stages. Does she ask a question to clarify her perception? Here, there was none. If she had continued being attentive, indicating that she wanted to hear a little more, I might have said something like this.

"The key reason I am writing this book is because of the transformative difference genuine dialogue makes in a person's life. The more it is practiced, the more mutual it becomes, the more one recognizes who one really is—not just an individual identity making decisions based on one's own thoughts and feelings, but a relational identity in which I become We by making decisions in consort with others' thoughts and feelings, being influenced by others' questions and responses."

Again, I listen attentively. If a person addresses me with a question or comment, especially with an advice-seeking question, I slow down before responding. Short of that, I might add other clarifying questions. Dialogue has changed my life. I used to search and study and travel and search and listen to wise teachers and search for knowledge, for awareness, for some kind of secret information that I would find and that would enlighten me to "the truth." As if I would know what to do with it, and then what to do with the next truth when the first truth no longer worked, I realized I would still be searching. Always searching, always feeling bad for something I had never realized.

And as the rhythm of searching and being disappointed with what was found—because "I" was the problem in the first place—rather than finding *it*, I was finally found by *it*. The it was a "dialogic awakening."

Deeply listening is not a game, not a technique, but, as Buber writes, "an obligation" to the person speaking. As a result, my life journey shifted. Of course I am not speaking here of a simple linear shift between two intellectual ideas. Ah, if only it were so easy. Rather, I am speaking here of different physical, intellectual, emotional, spiritual, psychological ways of living concretely in the world. You'll see. What's in this book is a transformative road map, one that continues to lead us beyond imprisoning ideas, ever again to the vital reciprocity as We.

"I" Exam

For years, I have been imprisoned by false ideas, by moments of reflexion—invisible bars that have stolen my mind. Something was missing in my life. It wasn't anything I could put my finger on. It certainly wasn't another idea, another book, another teacher, another another. That I knew. But what? That, I didn't know.

Still . . .

For too long, especially in my Buddhist years (my late twenties and early thirties) and then in my Catholic years (my late thirties, forties and fifties), I believed (wished) that some event, some awakening would seize me and resolve my anxieties. This would allow me to execute a spiritual blueprint especially designed to remodel my soul. All that I had to do was find the right blueprint. You may already see *my* problem here.

But there are many "right" blueprints. What I had to do was to just execute one. Failing that, it became apparent that I would have to start creating the blueprint myself. At first, I had sought out peak experiences, even though the late University of California, Santa Cruz Professor Donald Nicholl (in the old city of Jerusalem during Christmas of '85) once warned against the blindness of collecting these spiritual "experiences." I read book after book by enlightened masters or grace-filled mystics even though Bodhidharma, the presumptive founder of Zen, taught its basic principles as:

Not relying on words or letters;

An independent Self-transmitting apart from any teaching;

Directly pointing to Heart/Mind;

Awakening Original-Nature-actualizing Buddhahood.

As a late blooming hippie (though I never described myself that way), I tried applying transformational technologies from the human potential movement, to my life, but always with the same lack of success. Breakthroughs came, but they were followed (a week later, a month later) by the same breakdowns, the same anxieties I had felt before.

I sought out wise persons of intense interest (East and West) and interviewed them, later transcribing their words, putting some into books. Yet those words always remained someone else's insights, someone else's "truth."

I was looking in the *wrong places* for the *wrong thing* in the *wrong way*. In each situation, I remained separate and separable from the belief, from the practice. Whether Zen's no-self awakening, or Catholicism's living-and-dying with Christ, each remained stuck within the content of my own experience. I had overlooked of course, Dogen's advice: "We do not work to support our practice, our work is our practice."

And yet I could not resist looking. Without consciously realizing it, my conundrum was relentlessly pointing me toward *relationships* and calling me to take the day by the hand and practice *genuine dialogue*.

"My mistake," I once said in a class that I guest lectured for after I retired, "was not recognizing that 'I' had made a mistake from the beginning." My basic premise—my operational motive—was wrong. For the better part of two decades, across several continents, I was looking for what doesn't exist, pretending all the while that it did.

I was searching for "self-awareness" as if such a thing, such a truth, such an enlightenment existed independently of myself, as if I could realize it for/by myself. I had interpreted the awakened self through egocentric categories without first letting my egoistic individuality morph into relational personhood.

I created my own conundrum as a consequence: to live in and overlook the problem until it was forgotten. I had forgotten the vital distinction between "not knowing" and "not knowing that I didn't know." Forgotten, too, was the Bodhisattva's teaching: "I will not enter Nirvana until all sentient beings enter Nirvana."

After hearing me speak at San Jose State University about these wasted years, an innocent, enthusiastic, young man (an earlier me?) earnestly asked: "How can I avoid making your mistake?"

Wasting no words, yet full of hesitation, I said: "With the best intention, a little grace, and some luck." Even as I was saying this, I felt a gigantic NO arise in my consciousness. No, that's not right. There's no answer other than by making the mistakes yourself.

I shiver, now, recalling the sincere eyes and earnest voice of the young questioner.

Now I might offer a vastly different answer. Now I suggest temporarily forgetting yourself (not easy of course, yet possible) in order to practice compassionate listening, listening to everything being said until you become spontaneously and naturally drawn to respond to whatever or whomever is appropriate. One of my favorites is to ask a dialogue-deepening question like: "What's beneath that?" or "What else is important to know?"

And then more compassionate listening. Try that. "It's a listening process," as my teacher Professor Friedman once said.

Obedient Listening

"How can I prepare to enter dialogue?" asked a young philosophy professor after a class about Buber. He continued: "What does Buber say about how I should enter into relationships?" We can say that Buber would have answered directly that one cannot prepare for genuine dialogue except by fostering a willingness to listen.

While I could not have realized it at the time, his questions turn out to be a solid plank in the platform on which this book stands. Clearly, *Martin Buber's Dialogue* addresses the young teacher's questions by indicating that the more we practice the elements of genuine dialogue, the more we learn about how it works, the more we want to practice it.

I remember at the time that Buber would have certainly said, "There is nothing one can do to generate genuine dialogue in the moment, since it occurs through the grace in which two or more persons engage each other, each speaking as an act of their being and listening attentively and obediently to the other's words with meaning."

But obedient to whom?

This is an important question because we might (as I did when I first heard the term) immediately recoiling, assume the term refers to a person of authority. Rather, the term "obedient," as Buber uses it, refers to listening *attentively* to what the other person is saying, and for what is beneath what the other is saying.

Obedient listening refers to the listening process itself. According to Buber, this distinguishes itself from another form, active listening, which includes: having a reason or purpose for listening, suspending judgment, resisting distractions, pausing before responding, rephrasing the other's context in one's own words, and seeking out the feelings of the message.

"Obedient listening" includes: turning toward the other with one's whole being (body/mind/spirit), being fully present to the uniqueness of the situation with the other, faithfully and attentively responding, imagining what the other is thinking, feeling, perceiving, asking meaning-directed questions, and attending both to what is said and to what is not said.

Of course, it should be said that genuine listening is not always possible. Even if and when you are attentive, the other may be bringing anger or frustration from a prior context which prevents them from listening and legitimately responding.

The energy required, the interest maintained, the compassion necessary cannot be sustained. There are times when you are involved in a job or school-related project to the point of being exhausted.

Genuine listening is also made possible by a moment's relational grace, by a gift that has no rational, cognitive explanation.

Just as for Buber, one form of dialogue is really nothing more than monologue in disguise in which two or more people meeting in space speak each with themselves in a strangely tortuous and circuitous way. Another form of un-listening is hearing only what you think is being said or should be said. Often, it is brought about when you (as listener) deny the other's experience.

What is it that brings the other to say what they are saying? In fact, unlistening both causes monological speaking and misunderstanding, each terminating possibilities of genuine dialogue.

In pursuit of genuine dialogue, it is helpful to be attentive to times when you fail to listen deeply, especially when expecting the other person to be listening attentively to you.

Were you distracted? If so, what could you do to un-distract yourself? How can you increase your attention span? How about what helps me more than any other method—soft listening or clear-minded listening.

There are many different ways of listening. Listen to the way Buber listens—deeply, teachingly. Listen to the way the Zen master listens—quietly and teachingly.

The following brief but powerful event occurred when an American disciple brought his Zen master with him to Jerusalem, to visit the home of Martin Buber. In the center of the conversation,

> with great verve the American held forth that all religions were basically one, different variations on an identical theme, manifold manifestations of one and the same essence. Buber gave him one of his long, piercing looks, and then shot at him the question: "And what is the essence?" At this point the Zen master could not contain himself: he jumped from his seat and with both hands shook the hands of Buber.[1]

If the heart of dialogue requires the simple capacity to listen, then listening requires not only hearing what is said, but also preparing to listen. To put it another way, I've known many educators (and others) who prepare to speak, but very few who also prepare to listen. But why not?

Indian philosopher, Krishnamurti puts the challenge this way:

> I do not know if you have ever examined how you listen, it doesn't matter to what, whether to a bird, to the wind in the leaves, to the rushing waters, or how you listen in a dialogue with yourself, to your conversation in various relationships with your intimate

1. Mendes-Flohr, ed., *Martin Buber: A Contemporary Perspective*, 173.

friends, your wife or husband. If we try to listen, we find it extraordinarily difficult, because we are always projecting our opinions and ideas, our prejudices, our background, our inclinations, our impulses; when they dominate, we hardly listen at all. One listens and therefore learns, only in a state of attention, a state of silence, in which this whole background is abeyance, is quiet; then, it seems to me, it is possible to communicate.[2]

To prepare to listen is to replace at least temporarily our inner clamor with an inner silence. In other words, we need to create an opening, a quiet space, where listening and hearing can occur.

Here's a tip by William Isaacs, founder of the Dialogue Project at MIT:

Learning to listen begins with recognizing how you are listening now. Generally, we are not all that conscious of how we listen. You can begin to listen by listening first to yourself and to your own reactions. Ask yourself, What do I feel here? Or, How does this feel? Try to identify what you feel more carefully and directly. Beginning with the perception of your own feelings connects you to your heart and to the heart of your experience. To learn to be present, we must learn to notice what we are feeling now.[3]

Underlying listening is the principle of stillness. How does one act still? How can I cultivate a deep silence? Be centered. Be still. Stand still. Sit still. It seems to me that it all comes to finding a stillness within ourselves, a stillness that can be accessed when we are listening to another person speak.

Centering my attention allows me to stand quietly at the center of a turning world with whomever is present with me. Centering means finding a point of balance where I can accept the other as I accept myself.

Centering is finding a balancing point, a point of quiet within oneself. It is not static, nor placid, but pliable and fluid. It is not imagined, but realistic. From this place, real listening occurs.

One doesn't often have an opportunity to look back into one's life to see more clearly and recognize more succinctly where and when an invaluable

2. Jiddu Krishnamurti, *Talks and Dialogues*, quoted in Isaacs, *Dialogue and the Art of Thinking Together*, 84.

3. Isaacs, *Dialogue and the Art of Thinking Together*, 92.

life-long lesson was first learned. In my case, the teacher was my mother; and the lesson was vigilant listening. The lesson took place in a Philadelphia Baptist Church after the Sunday morning service had ended.

Frances was my mother's conversational as well as choir mate. Without fail, Frances, a forty-year-old brunette spinster still living with her mother (who insisted she remain at home to help her out), would remain after church each Sunday to talk with my mother.

What Frances wanted, more than anything else, was to be married. "If only, if only," I can still hear her saying. "If only I could be married . . ." And on and on. I could always count on her having more of the same thing to say in the same way about her same feelings.

I would stand in the choir loft, off to the side, hungry and hungrier. But Frances always had more to say, more of the same thing, Sunday after Sunday, week after week.

It was a late fall morning and I was walking home from church with my mother as I always did after Sunday morning service. But this day was different. A question arose that confused my boyish mind. Why? Why had my mother continued to do what she did? "Why," I asked her as we walked, "do you listen to Frances that way?" Now and then I kicked up small piles of orange/red/brown leaves blown into little sidewalk piles by gusting winds.

I waited. "How come you never say anything? How come Frances does all the talking?" It seems completely "unfair," was the word I used. "She does all the talking, all the time. How come?"

Are you ready for what came back to me? I certainly wasn't! I've never forgotten it. She said: "Some people just need you to listen to them because no one else does. They just need someone to listen to them—just listen. So I listen. That's what she needs the most."

What I remember, what I have never forgotten (even though I never fully understood it) is that there are people (all of us?) who just need to be listened to, to be heard, *really* heard.

Being a young boy who was hungry and bored, witnessing such an encounter between my mom and Frances—who wasn't even my mother's friend—for that fifteen minutes seemed like an overbearing asking. Why, I continued to ask myself. Why?

Distracted by Distractions

In T. S. Eliot's *Four Quartets*, the poet describes in "Burnt Norton" the one thing that most interrupts our attentive listening to one another: "We are distracted from distraction by distractions." Bang. That's certainly not a whisper. Few of us, especially in our time, would have difficulty understanding Eliot's brilliant insight—that even our questions, let alone our listening, is distracted.

Diversions lurk everywhere in ways that interrupt attentive listening, without which there is no real dialogue. Without deeply listening to the other, there is only, as William Blake wrote, "Mind-forged manacles," or monologue.

This morning, for instance, I watched two new University of California, Santa Cruz students meeting in the foyer outside the pool. I was sitting off to the side and remained unnoticed. As they exchanged ideas and responses back and forth, I watched the way their tall bodies stood and shifted, the way each of them gestured with their arms and hands. I carefully watched their eyes.

One, the younger student, instead of looking straight at the other, looked off to the side and down while speaking. Meanwhile, the other student looked more directly into the face of the person with whom he was speaking. Back and forth they went, first excitedly and then the excitement waned and they each went on their way.

I couldn't help wonder, as I sat watching the two students walk away, if the one who looked directly at the other while speaking wasn't a bit distracted by the other's looking down and away while speaking. I know I would have been.

And I wondered if the downward sideway-glancing young man did so because he was distracted. And if so, by what? Was it something in the environment? Was it something internal; or was it habitual? I can't know of course. What I do know, however, is if I were speaking with him, I would have been distracted.

Some distractions are easy to spot—noises, sirens, your iPhone. Many distractions are assumed to be external threats, random and stupid nagging at us: device notifications, extra-loud advertisements, pointless meetings, small talk. These are distractions that pry our attention away from what we have been paying attention to.

Other distractions, of course, are less frivolous, yet no less deframing our attention and focus; distractions such as cognitive failures, byproducts of sugar or artificial colors, or video games, or brain chemistry, or social media.

Almost as soon as I began naming some of the things that distract us, I realized you could do a better job at listing them than I could. And everybody's list would be unique to them. Still, it might be good to make a list of distractions and then post it where it can be seen as a reminder of what might interrupt the flow of dialogue.

And if you remember, remember any of this—remember your eyes. Your eyes are beautiful, not to be hidden. Your eyes are expressive. Turning away from yourself and toward the other and addressing the other, warmly and openly, it is your eyes that invite him/her into conversation. Your eyes are beautiful, your eyes are expressive. We listen with our eyes.

Dialogic Awakening

The year was 1995. In the fall, an inquisitive lady with short hair and a radiant smile came to my class. It was the German-born Mechthild.

Mechthild is a woman who is not afraid to be wrong because she has no stake in being right. And she is an accomplished listener, which is no small achievement. She has raised three children in Germany and then in America.

Oh yes, and she cares for and supports family still living in Germany plus a growing number of friends in America. She is a woman who honestly would rather give, and give more, than receive. Being mildly disingenuous, as I often was, I recognized that one rarely meets such a genuine person. She is, I would discover, both open-minded and open-hearted, giving and forgiving. And—most importantly—a listener's listener.

The lady with the radiant smile who had a talent for listening was so intellectually curious that she talked to me after class many times. In our discussions, she recognized "something genuine" in me just beneath my various masks.

She had come into my class because she wanted to discuss dreams that she had in which a favorite Aunt in Germany was visiting her after dying. She shared stories with me of her childhood in Germany: of standing up against her lawyer father's anger; of running away and hiding from her parents; of giving her last money away to a friend in need; and of living within a fantastic dream-like imagination.

She spoke with an open heart, as if there was no agenda between us. She held nothing back and would not accept it when I did. We discussed Ultimacy. At the time I was a practicing Catholic. She practiced the divinity of every moment. I said it was important to raise your children in a tradition, to give them something to rebel against. She said it was important to teach your children many traditions so that they can choose their own way.

One day, she brought a friend who was visiting from India to meet me in my office before class. She had mentioned this earlier to me. They came. Fine, but I continued talking to another teacher who was there before them. She and her guest sat and waited until it was too late. It was time for the next class.

Our next conversation, and the one thereafter, came to a screeching halt. She asked me—face-to-face, eyes-to-eyes—for an apology before our dialogue could proceed.

I knew better than to say, as I had before, "That's just the way I am!" And I knew, in fact, that only honesty would be accepted.

When I was alone, I conjectured many rationalizations. I told myself, only half-heartedly, that I was ultimately right. It wasn't my fault. I had to do what I did in the way I did it. But none of these explanations would she accept. "We cannot go forward in our relationship," she insisted, "until we get through this bypass."

Stuck again.

Soon thereafter, sitting in my blue two-wheel drive Jeep before my "Death, Dying, and Religions" class, we were discussing our roadblock. I said to her, "You have disappointed me." I could not let go of my overwhelming need to be right in this (and every) situation.

She listened carefully. She responded: "No! You can be angry at me, you can be furious with me, but never disappointed because that means you expect me to match a fanciful image that is in your mind. I'll never be that." These words shook my hardheaded middle-aged brain. She was right, and I could only resolve the problem dialogically—person to person.

This came as a breakthrough insight that I knew on arrival to be true. Arising from the space between us, an invisible grace freed my ongoing resistance. Being mutual trumps being right!

I said to her, from a place deep inside, "I couldn't agree more." I reached across the space between us and hugged her, silently, deeply.

Mechthild remains my closest, dearest, most genuine dialogical partner. She is real and challenges me to keep it real.

I took this encounter with Mechthild to wake me from the slumber of a deeply rooted ignorance. This is why I have deliberately used the term "awakening." It marks not only the shift from individualism to mutuality, but, even more importantly, from knowledge about dialogue to practicing it. Looking out, at last, through practicing eyes and really seeing/hearing the otherness of the other renews, for me, life's unmediated splendor right here, right now, always between us.

The Delivery Man

As usual, he came round to the back door. He is tall, thin, silver-haired in jeans, sneakers, his short-sleeved green delivery shirt with the name of the drugstore sewn on his shirt pocket. Each time he came, he rescued me from sitting at my desk, alone, writing words intended to spark intelligent conversations about a better way of living than living looking for a better way.

The delivery man brings soul in his bright, sun-filled smile and life experience stories. He stands in the doorway and immediately, without trying, attracts full attention. When I ask myself why, right away it's obvious. The energy of his voice is captivating. His words, and the way he delivers them, is as if he could in any moment break out into laughter.

This time, however, he brought an announcement. He was retiring. Although he was already retired, now this would make it his second retirement.

"Why now?" I ask with a touch of sadness in that his monthly visits always lifted my spirits.

"Because it became obvious that it wasn't taking me anywhere. I took the job to get some extra spending money but it wasn't working. But that's another story," he said as if I didn't need to know it.

As we continued talking, he shifted the bag he brought from one hand to the other.

"What will you do?" Since I too am retired, I'm always interested in hearing different answers to that question.

"Well, I've got to clean up the house, fix things, relax. And I've planned a few bike rides."

"How far do you ride in a day?"

"About 500 miles is a good amount and that allows us to keep our speed around 50 mph. I want to see the country as I go." I could see how much he was already riding his motorcycle in his mind.

We continued talking and listening and talking. A sparkle was in his eye as he told me "the other story" behind the silver-haired, late 70s delivery man's finally quitting his job. "I took it just to earn some extra spending money beyond my pension. It turned out, however," he said in his short-sleeve green delivery shirt, "that I was just making enough to pay off my wife's credit cards."

"Oh no," I responded, "That's like losing the radio station, when the one you always listen to turns to static. It's good that you caught it."

"I have to thank my oldest daughter for helping me out. It used to be that by the week's end, I was exhausted," he laughed.

This is the shortened version of "the other story" that first he indicated he wouldn't tell me, then he did. Why?

I didn't ask him to, I just listened attentively as I do whenever he comes to everything he says. And one thing he was saying led to the next—his wife's lies, his upcoming road trip, his special delivery routes, and times ("like you, always after three PM, always through back door"). Why did he continue telling me so much?

In that moment, I was a good listener, attentive and curious and interested and following everything said.

Almost all of us have some form of communication problem which keeps us from being fully attentive. That or what it is, yet it doesn't take a communications specialist to recognize that the problem would be less problematic if a person *listened deeply* to the other more attentively, more openly.

Here's why.

I must admit that Buber grasped my attention to "obedient listening" by at first driving me away with the term "obedient." But that was before I compared it a more popularized form of listening today, active listening.

These are the days when we are reminded again that the past does not remain in the past. We bring it along with us, if our eyes are really open. In this case, it's the incidental note that gives us the most telling image, an intricate and absorbing, yet unknown image of a world-renowned writer and thinker that completely justifies his reputation.

Early 1952 found Buber and his wife Paula of all places in Los Angeles, California. While in his first visit to America, he was invited to teach for two months at the University of Judaism, the west coast branch of the Jewish Theological Seminary. Buber was very interested in meeting the next generation of Jewish teachers, as well as seeing the western-most edge of America. As Maurice Friedman tells us:

> Once in Los Angeles, when Buber was traveling some distance in a taxi, the taxi driver suddenly turned to him and said, "Mister, I've got something to ask you. The other day, I read that you don't have to get angry right away. What do you think about that?"
>
> Buber asked him where he had read it. "In a magazine," the taxi driver replied. "Don't laugh, but the guy who said it is seven hundred years old."
>
> "You mean he lived seven hundred years ago?" Buber asked.
>
> "Yeah, that's what I said. Name of Francis . . . Francis? . . . Oh yes, Francis of Assisi."
>
> "Oh then you have read something good," said Buber, and told him about Saint Francis of Assisi. After paying and departing, Buber missed his eyeglass case and decided that the handsome case must have fallen out of his pocket in the cab. Twenty minutes later, as he was coming out of the building, he encountered the cab driver walking toward him, with the case in his hand.
>
> As Buber himself pointed out in telling the story, for such a driver's time is money and gasoline is more money. Recognizing that, Buber said to him, "Thank you. That was good of you. You are a very nice man."
>
> At this, the giant of a man put his arms around the diminutive Buber and declared, "Nobody has ever said that to me before."[4]

That's because, I would say, no one had ever really listened to him before. Buber listened obediently whether it was to Eliot or a cab driver.

Boldly (Empathically) Swinging

Attentive listening involves more than hearing—both what is said and what is not said. It also involves an act of imagination.

Experiencing the other's side in a dialogical relationship is at the core of interhuman relationships. The act of truly encountering another person

---

4. Friedman, *My Friendship with Martin Buber*, 52

usually involves our imagining what the other is feeling, thinking, and experiencing without giving up the felt reality of one's own activity. This may seem almost contradictory. Necessarily, we must hold onto our own ground of subjectivity to be human, we also are called to go forth and meet the other. Thus, we live in a kind of tension or on a narrow ridge between the "I" and the "other."

Buber writes:

> Some call it intuition, but that is not a wholly unambiguous con-cept. I prefer the name 'imagining the real', for in its essential being this gift is not a looking at the other but boldly swinging—de-manding the most intensive stirring of one's being—into the life of the other.[5]

This means, seeing through the eyes of another and experiencing the other's side as if from one's own side without ceasing to experience one's own stand. What is required is a willing imagination, a temporary suspen-sion of one-sided thinking and experiencing.

The capacity to boldly swing to the other side involves two nearly si-multaneous movements: 1) empathically imagining the other's side, and 2) bringing *back* to my own side as much of the other situation as I can glean, not as detached content, but as living process.

Buber often talked about the practice of empathy, however not by that name. Here's why. By the term "empathy" people of his time often meant experiencing from the other's side by surrendering one's own stand. Not so for Buber. One surrenders their stand (positioning, world view) at most only temporarily. Then he takes it up again.

Buber writes:

> This is the nature of all genuine imagining, only that here the realm of my action is not the all-possible, but the particular real person who confronts me, whom I can attempt to make present to myself just in this way, and not otherwise, in his wholeness, unity, and uniqueness, and with his dynamic centre which realizes all these things ever new.[6]

Though I cannot become another person, I can go as far as possible to experience our relationship through the other person's perspective. This process is made all the more important because my responses are

---

5. Buber, *The Knowledge of Man*, 81.
6. Ibid.

influenced in turn by the other's perspectives, which I have brought back to my side.

When I speak empathically, the person to whom I am speaking feels heard, feels understood, feels more willing to be honest, to share intimate details of their life with you, to really want to listen to what you have to say.

Landauer's Murder: Buber's Silence

Stranger than most events in this book, this episode recounts one of the rare times when Buber had nothing to say, nothing. His best friend had been tortured and kicked to death on the way from one prison to another after being arrested on false charges over his political stand. Buber, the thinker and writer, had nothing to say.

Gustav Landauer—Buber's closest friend and authentic political and socialist revolutionary—is the one whose "dark charism" forced him to take a stand against the government that was cracking down on individual freedoms prior to World War I. Anarchist and pacifist, Landauer was, without question, the single most important influence on Buber's thinking and writing in the early 1900s.

Even though Landauer and Buber held significantly different social and political views, their ever-deepening friendship was anchored, from Buber's side at least, in their dialogical conversations. They challenged each other, disagreeing as well as agreeing with each other. After one such conversation, Landauer wrote Buber:

> Despite all your protestations, I am obliged to call [your attitude to the war] a species of aestheticism and formalism. Moreover, I say that you . . . have no right whatsoever to join the public debate over the political events of the present which is called the World War and to order this chaos into your beautiful and wise generalities; what emerges is something wholly untenable and revolting . . . I must admit, my blood boils when I read [what you have written.]

And:

> You deny precisely that which is most essential through the employment of your vacuous method: you contemplate the everyday and declare it a wonder; you do not encounter the everyday with a formative vision; rather, you attempt to dovetail it into your schemata.[7]

7. Letter dated May 12, 1916, sent from Landauer to Buber, in *The Letters of Martin*

Landauer's rebuke stunned Buber, yet he soon argued, similar to Landauer, that spiritual change must be preceded by a transformation of relationship between persons.

Landauer's pacifist resistance to the war (in the days of postwar chaos) was even more radical than Buber's own, but Buber was devastated by the news of Landauer's death. Soldiers of the Third Reich beat, kicked, and finally murdered him in the Stadelheim prison where he was taken for questioning. Friedman writes:

> Buber's response to the news of Landauer's death was probably, next to his 'conversion' and the early separation from his mother, the most important single event in his life. Yet this is one 'autobiographical fragment' that Buber could not write. When I urged him to do so in Jerusalem in 1960, he confessed he had tried and found himself still too close to this event to be able to write about it.[8]

On receiving news of Landauer's barbaric murder, Buber reported that he was compelled to imagine this killing, not only visually, but with his *body*. In response to this event, Buber was called to feel in his own body every blow that Landauer had suffered in that courtyard where he had been beaten to death.

But why, you may be wondering, do I recount such a horrific story at the end of this chapter?

Talk about the need for empathy, about imagining what another person is feeling, thinking, experiencing, with emphasis on "feeling," can you even imagine what Buber was called to do? Moreover, can you imagine being so deeply impacted by a friend's murder that you would . . .

Practicing Listening

After coming this far, practicing listening comes naturally. We can't stop now. Why would we want to? No, having come this far, having practiced *turning* and *addressing*, now I really want to discover what the other person is saying, what they want me to hear.

Think of what an honor, what a privilege it is to hear what another person really wants to tell you, to illustrate, to convince you of, and to teach you.

Buber, 188.

8. Friedman, *Encounter on the Narrow Ridge*, 114.

Just think: listening co-creates your speaking. I am called/invited to say things that, in retrospect, come even as a surprise to me. Listening attentively, listening deeply, naturally elicits creative responses.

Listening is not only the issue. We wake up listening. The main concern is to whom should I listen? I suggest listening to those who really listen to you. Listen to a good listener.

To start with, check in with your listening habits. We all have them. What are yours? How do you prevent yourself from hearing everything that is said, even what is implied? What habitual behaviors block you from listening?

Try listening as a way of getting started. Even though you may still catch yourself listening judgmentally, and associatively (as I far too often do) shift to paying deep attention as quickly as you can. Try it: catch yourself and shift, catch yourself and pay full attention. Notice how different your listening becomes.

Here's a way to portray it:

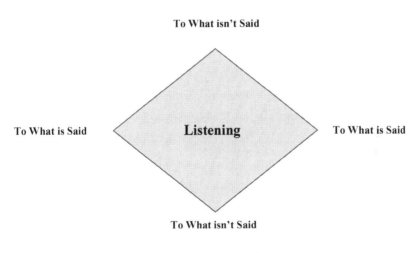

Listening Deeply

To What Is Said

- Openly and receptively even when the other disagrees with your viewpoints
- Without analyzing, associating, or judging the other person

To What Isn't Said

- What is inferred beneath the spoken or unspoken words
- By boldly swinging to the other's side to imaginatively feel, think, experience what the other is feeling, thinking, experiencing

Buber speaks of a person genuinely listening to the other, with full attention. Everyone who listens in this way is listening with one's specific, definitive, personal existence. It is only possible to make someone fully present by concentrating all your attention, all your energy, all your interests upon how that person is able to listen to you and what that person has to say.

Here, it is crucial to understand that in order to listen fully to the other, it is necessary to become aware not only of what the other says through our senses, but what they are thinking and feeling and experiencing at that moment. Listening is not just a part of human nature, a part of social ritual, a part of family rites of passage, but a very intimate interaction between specific persons who willingly trust the process of dialogue.

4

Responding

The Nurse with a New Hairstyle

A VISITING NURSE CAME to see me one morning after I had just had my first sip of organic coffee. Feeling lively, I intercepted her routine and pivoted it toward the following question. It was a question that I assumed would generate a little discussion: "With whom do you have the most meaningful dialogue?"

She smiled. As she did, she turned her head away from me. I noticed that she had a different look than usual. "Did you do something different with your hair," I asked. "Yes," she said, "I spent an extra 15 minutes with my hair this morning before leaving for work." "Well," I said, "It looks very nice." "Thank you," she said with a delicate smile forming on her lips.

"But now I don't want you to forget my question. 'With whom do you have the most meaningful dialogue?'"

"Who are you talking about?" she said.

"The world," I answered, somewhat surprised at her question. I said this not to exclude anyone in her life, rather to include everyone who might be a good dialogical partner.

She paused and clearly shifted her energy into conscious thought "Hmm . . . , Well, my sister and I." At that point, she interrupted herself. "With my husband, of course."

"What is it about those dialogues, the ones you have with your husband, that make them the most meaningful?" I responded. I could think of several reasons why a person would answer that way, but I wanted to see what her reasons were. She had already told me once she had only been married for about five years and also that she had a three-year-old son.

"The question answers itself, doesn't it," she immediately retorted "Yes, the question can answer itself."

"But can you tell me what you mean by that?" I asked, sensing that we could be at the beginning of a stream of conversation that would take us into a slightly different domain.

"Your question is the answer; communication connects us." Seeing that I was eager to continue the dialogue, she immediately preformed her own pivot and pulled out her necessary nursing accessories in order to test my oxygen intake, my blood pressure, and my heartbeat. "I am a visiting nurse after all, not a philosopher like you," she said.

A Confirming Dialogue

According to Buber, there's no genuine dialogue without wholeheartedly *turning*, and *addressing* the other. Similarly there can be no genuine dialogue without attentively *listening* and responsibly *responding* to the other.

Perhaps the greatest dialogues, Buber discovered, as I have, are ones that include the yet to occur, the kind that leave no seams between its partners, the kind that are timeless in a non-mystical way. Such conversations are effortless to slip into because they bring with them the implicit promise made by each of the partners in former dialogues—a confirmation that each person will be fully present and available in and for future dialogues.

Confirmation of the other is one of the most valuable gifts given to dialogical partners. Naturally following acceptance and affirmation, confirmation means that you will continue to accept and affirm the other in future engagements.

As dialogical persons, we enter ever anew into a flowing interchange of addressing and responding, of confirming and being confirmed. It is here at this point that our unique wholeness becomes manifested.

But wait. When I confirm another person, according to Buber, in myself and in them, I am not just confirming them exactly as they are, but also in and through their potentiality—in what that person is meant to become. I/We bring the future into the present.

We all need to be confirmed as unique persons, persons we are and/or may become. Buber sums up its significance of what has been said in this section as follows:

> Sent forth from the natural domain of species into the hazard of
> the solitary category, surrounded by the air of a chaos which came
> into being with him, then secretly and bashfully he watches for
> a Yes which allows him to be and which can come to him only

from one man to another. It is from one person to another that the
heavenly bread of self-being is passed.[1]

Re-read that last sentence. It provides a lyrical description of what
could be called sacramental dialogue, in which the transcendent bread of
self-being of each person's sustaining self-identity, each person's unique
wholeness is shared. Thus dialogue, when genuine, says "Yes" to the hu-
manity of each person.

He came at 11:10 on a sunny, cool morning. I remember the time's exact-
ness because normally I am at the UC gym at that time. Instead, on that
morning I was sitting at my desk working on this manuscript when the
front doorbell rang.

Aaron, my son-in-law, answered. I barely heard the visitor announce
himself as "a long lost friend."

"Ken," Aaron called out from the front door, "There's someone here
who says he is a long lost friend of yours."

"Here I come," I called back. "Let him in." Cluelessly and curious I
rode out toward the front door where a tall, thin, bespeckled stranger stood.

"Time has ravaged our bodies," he said, looking at me. I still didn't
recognize him. He had the appearance of a seriously significant face, the
memory of whom would not be far behind.

Then, all at once, he extended his hand which I brushed aside in order to reach up and hug him. "Demetrious." The stranger was Demetrious
whom I had last seen more than twenty years ago at a bookshop where I
gave a talk on my *Death Dreams* book. Demetrious was the contractor who
had helped our family expand our first California house by saying he could
refunction a eucalyptus trunk sitting in a nearby gulch by cutting it loose,
dragging it up to the house, and using it as a center pole planted in concrete
which would support the new second floor.

"And you let me do it," he said to me, as if questioning to this day the
possibility of pulling it off, crazy as it was.

As we talked, timelessly, the subject of "dialogue" arose. He knew I
had written several books on Buber. "You know," he said, "dialogue doesn't
always need words."

---

1. Buber, *The Knowledge of Man*, 71.

"Yes, sometimes just a glance is all that is needed. Dialogue can occur in complete silence."

"When I first met you in the late 70s," Demetrious said, "I remember having a wordless dialogue with you, after which I knew I could always trust you."

And here we are after all these years, still knowing, each of us, still feeling that trust, that respect for one another, which continues with us and brings us right here, right today into these words.

I didn't quote these words because it's as each of us, together, said them, each of us—having not seen each other for more than twenty years— together understood them.

"What Do You Think?" Buber Asked

Mishael Caspi, the late Professor in the Department of Philosophy and Religious Studies at Bates College, Maine, exemplified what is being said about the constituents of listening attentively and responding responsibly in his personal account of meeting Buber for the first time:

> My earliest memory of Professor Martin Buber was at a seminar he gave in the teacher training college which he created in the fifties in Israel. I remember in a class of about seven or eight, he talked about the book of Genesis and the creation of the world. With his smiling eyes and white beard, he talked in a way that bewildered me. Sometimes, I felt what he was saying was much beyond me.
>
> At one point, he said something about his concept of creation which I did not fully understand. I raised my hand and he stopped talking and asked me what I wanted to say. "I would very much like to know what is your conception of the creation of the world." And try to understand, while I was raised in a very orthodox house, I had just finished my service in the army. Being a member of the Kibutz, I was between Orthodoxy and a denial of all its teaching. So I really wanted to understand how other people view the creation.
>
> In a very beautiful Jewish way he said to me: "What is creation for you?" I looked at him with surprise at the fact that he wanted to know from me what I wanted to know from him. I stuttered at first, and then I said: "I think that creation is to be a part of what is happening, a part of creation." And he shook his head and said, "No, no, no! It is to be together *with* creation." It took me a long time to be able to understand the difference between "to be a part

of" and "to be a part *with.*" In many senses I understood later on that Buber's response emphasized for me the whole concept of *I and Thou* in a very simple way.

By crossing over to Caspi's side of their meeting, by concretely imagining what he was thinking and feeling, Buber gained insight into the situation of Mishael's question that, in turn, led him to question the questioner and cut to the heart of the matter. Buber's practice of responding responsibly allowed him to provide an answer that would continue to flower in Mishael's understanding and open for him the fruitfulness of address.

The impact of Buber's response underscored his question. To answer God's question, "Where are you?" Buber would reply, "Right here, right now, taking a dialogical stand."

Buber maintains that dialogue, finally, is not a subjective activity. It does not just arise from one's own efforts. Instead, it arises as the result of mutual concern between human beings. Really seeing the other is finally possible only when there is some form of relational reciprocity and equality between them. And this is possible to the extent that I am willing to pass beyond subjective experiencing in order to make the other present as he or she alone.

Dialogical relationships, therefore, reach their highest perfection in "being present," grounded in a capacity for holding before one's soul a reality arising in the moment that cannot be personally contained.

Mutual Animated Describing

Though infrequently mentioned, Buber's relationship to his wife Paula was of crucial importance for his life's work. In the summer of 1899, while attending the University of Zurich, Buber met Paula Winkler, and they married shortly after, over objections that she was a Gentile, "a pagan," as she joked. Although raised a Munich Catholic, she converted to Judaism, and in so doing lost her own family. Yet, remarkably, as Hugo Bergmann observed, when Paula said, "we Jews," "he felt confirmed."

Paula was a woman given to an enormous amount of intellectual energy and physical work. Friends related, and Buber understood, that she was in many ways emotionally stronger and more mature than Buber, and possessed an impressive intellect and poetic talent, acquiring a reputation as a writer and poet under the pseudonym Georg Munk. In Paula, Martin found true equality of relationship. And with Paula, Buber came to recognize that a marriage is built not upon feelings, but upon relational respect and trust.

Along with Buber, Paula became an enthusiastic participant in helping to create a life of community and dialogue. In a way, Buber regained his missing mother in Paula. She lent him strength and emotional support and direction for his unharnessed creative energies. Friedman writes:

> To grasp the full significance of Buber's approach to love and marriage in *I and Thou,* we must first speak of his relationship to his wife Paula—an influence probably more decisive for his I–Thou philosophy than any of the events or meetings that we have discussed. Buber's dialogical thinking could have grown only out of his marriage to this strong and really "other" woman, this modern Ruth who left her family, home, and religion, and finally even her country and people, for him. The fundamental reality of the life of dialogue—that is a confirmation and inclusion of otherness—was understood and authenticated in the love and the marriage, the tension and the companionship of his relationship to Paula.[2]

While his mother's disappearance came to signify the crucial "mismeeting" of Buber's life, his marriage to Paula was the crucial meeting, and restored his trust in the eternal possibility of genuine relationships. One catches glimpses of Martin and Paula's relationship through their letters. Their early letters (collected in *The Letters of Martin Buber*) are intense, honest, encouraging, silly, and deeply loving. On August 14, 1899, Paula wrote:

> Sweet, dear, You must not start worrying immediately when a letter does not reach you . . . I do earnestly ask that of you. I have fond feelings for your great work—I would never want to spoil it for but I would like to slip myself between you and the little everyday bothers, like a sheltering cloud. That is why I so wish I were with you.[3]

And on November 17, 1901, she wrote:

> Dearest Mowgli,
>
> Mowgli dear, you were lovable in your last little note. It has filled me with courage and joy again, dearest. Yes, of course, dear heart, I

2. Friedman, *Martin Buber's Life and Work,* vol. 1, 336.
3. Buber, *Letters of Martin Buber,* 66.

love you beyond anything. And the good days when we'll feel that properly from heart to heart, they're just beginning, my only one.[4]

The significance of Buber's trust in Paula's good judgment and advice is evident in a letter he wrote to her on October 25, 1901 during a spell of depression:

> Dear Heart, Your letter may well be the right answer to mine. It certainly has pushed me hard. There is one thing you cannot understand, dearest: that every moment here I am struggling with every fiber of my being to bear up against all my restlessness, against all my cares, against all my knowledge, against all my deprivation, against everything that is trying to crush me. Every moment. And that your letters are the only source of strength for me . . .[5]

As these letters suggest, it was with Paula that Buber first came to realize and articulate the "mutual meeting" that characterized the spirit between them. Paula's strength, her integrity, and her responsibility are movingly celebrated in a poem that Buber wrote to her on her 50th birthday, "On the Day of Looking Back." Buber ends the poem with a powerful acknowledgment and confirmation of his wife:

> You element and woman,
>
> Soul and nature![6]

In a later poem, "Do You Still Know It?," Buber credits Paula with helping him find direction for his talents and interests. In it, he wrote two lines that link responding responsibly with "genuine dialogue":

> How a mutual animated describing
>
> Arose out of it and lived between you and me![7]

The phrase "mutual animated describing" points directly to the interhuman realm of "the between." In an alternative version of the poem, Paul Mendes-Flohr translates these key words to read, "a mutually moving portrayal."[2]

Compare these different translations of the "between": "A mutual animated describing," and "a mutually moving portrayal." The "between" is

4. Ibid., 79–80.

5. Ibid.

6. Buber, *Believing Humanism,* 49.

7. Ibid., 51.

thus a two-sided, oscillating human image emerging from Buber's relationship with Paula.

It helps me immensely at this point in our study to make another comparison—one between Buber's lyrical description of the between as "mutually animated describing" and his philosophical rhetoric depicting the same dialogical event between person and person. As a third voice in *Between Man and Man*, Buber writes:

> In the most powerful moments of dialogue, where in truth "deep calls unto deep," it becomes unmistakably clear that it is not the wand of the individual or of the social, but of a third [alternative] which draws the circle round the happening. On the far side of this subjective, on the side of the objective, on the narrow ridge, where you and I meet, there is the realm of the "between."[8]

The between is "there," a "mutual animated describing" arising where/when we enter into timeless dialogue with others, where/when the eternal listens and echoes us back to ourselves, back to I and You as not two, not one, there, where we are reciprocally mutual.

And here is the problem: the "between" is an invisible oscillating sphere. It is not a physical place:

• Not just a physical space between us;

• Not just the sum of everything passing between us.

Rather, the "between" is a reciprocal presence:

• The interhuman spirit of mutuality alive between, within, and around practitioners of genuine dialogue;

• The transcending third voice, not-one, not-two, the voice of genuine dialogue itself.

It's tempting to say that if you don't love chemistry, you've missed something essential about what makes life worth living. When I was an undergraduate, I took a required chemistry class. Studying chemistry was always difficult for me; yet it taught me one thing. I could not forget how two completely separate and discrete elements could together produce a third,

---

8. Buber, *Between Man and Man*, 204.

yet a completely different, reality. You remember: when two molecules of hydrogen are combined under the right conditions with a single molecule of oxygen, a new substance is produced—water.

Only later would I learn that what makes the appearance of the third reality—water—mysterious, is that both hydrogen and oxygen, by themselves, can be combustible, flammable. Yet without water resulting from two molecules of hydrogen and one of oxygen, we couldn't live.

Why do I mention this chemical interaction here? So that you will consider the possibility of an analogy. Instead of two different chemical elements, think now of two separate subjective intelligences with discrete passions coming together. Analogously, it can be said, as Buber discovered in his life with Paula, that under the right conditions human interaction produces a third reality—the *between*.

The between is not experienced by just one side of the relationship. Rather, it is mutually produced by relational interactions, altered by what each person experiences and expresses. Neither of the relational partners can generate the between alone; we can only attempt to create the conditions for its appearance. It is produced by a relational event.

Buber further writes, as we have seen, that analogous to water being released from chemical interactions, the between results from interpersonal relationships, as with Paula. Here's the result: to the extent that we enter into the between, we (each of us) become authentically human. Genuine dialogue thus leads to the ontological space of the between, from which our true humanness emerges.

Peter and Paul

The context for this crucially significant discussion is Buber's distinction between two types of persons: 1) the person who proceeds from the one he or she really is; 2) and the other proceeds from how he or she wishes to be perceived. This distinction is most significantly at work for Buber in the interhuman realm—in our personal interactions with one another in which we speak from our self-being. We speak truthfully; we are our words.

As Buber writes: "His look is 'spontaneous', 'without reserve'; of course he is not uninfluenced by the desire to make [him or herself] understood by the other, but he is uninfluenced by any thought of the idea of [him or herself] which he can or should awaken in the person whom he is looking at."[9]

9. Buber, *The Knowledge of Man*, 76.

However, and this is a huge however, when a person is more interested in how they sound when speaking, or how they appear, more concerned with their own image, this prevents genuine dialogue from occurring.

Imagine two corporate advisors on different boards of directors in the Silicon Valley. Imagine these men—Peter and Paul—living a life of sitting and talking in ways dominated by their appearance. Think about the different configurations which can take shape. For Buber, there are six:

1. Peter as he wishes to appear to Paul, and Paul as he wishes to appear to Peter;

2. Peter as he really appears to Paul, that is Paul's image of Peter;

3. Paul as he really appears to Peter, that is Peter's image of Paul;

4. Peter as he appears to himself, and Paul as he appears to himself;

5. The bodily Peter, and the bodily Paul;

6. Together Peter and Paul as two living beings and six imagistic appearances gathered in conversation between the two of them.

Considering this configuration, Buber asks, "Where is there room for any genuine interhuman life?"[10]

And of course, as Buber well knows, there is none. All the room is taken up by images. There is no room for self-being.

For this reason, according to Buber, "By far the greater part of what is today called conversation among [persons] would be more properly and precisely described as *speechifying*."[11] Speechifying—what an amazingly dissatisfying word. It suggests political-speak, to me, that is pre-planned speech for a designated effect. Indeed, as Buber remarks, one can hear in speechifying's the voice of one's own "suppressed longing."[12]

Therefore, the chief presupposition for authentic dialogue is accepting the other and making her or him present just as they really are, naturally and spontaneously in their true being.

10. Ibid., 77.
11. Ibid., 78, italics are mine.
12. Ibid., 79.

Again we come to Peter and Paul—this time as they really are image-free, as they are without seeming to be what they're not. Unlike before, imagine this time both Peter and Paul, because of something they've read either by Buber or about Buber, or because of the influence of someone they've met found it more and more impossible to be represented by an image.

For both Peter and Paul, their will to enter dialogical relationships—exactly as they are (and nothing else) has been stirred and strengthened.

Peter and Paul have come into genuine dialogue through the forces of real life, by the mutual power of personally making the other person present, by the vanishing of all semblances, and through the depths of a personal life call to each of them.

Peter, who is an avid reader, especially of philosophical texts, had come upon a yard sale in which a retired professor of philosophical literature was selling all of his paperback books for fifty cents or five for two dollars. From one box, Peter scooped up five Martin Buber books: *I and Thou, Between Man and Man, The Knowledge of Man, A Believing Humanism,* and *Pointing the Way.* This two-dollar investment, he would later learn, contained many of the books central to Buber's dialogical philosophy.

Paul, on the other hand, had come to meet a German-speaking lady who told him childhood stories of her family's discussing Buber's dialogical teaching at the dinner table. As Paul and his new friend grew to know each other better, Paul also began reading about Buber's teaching of dialogue and what made it so different.

It was a clear blue sky, sunny warm mid-winter day when Peter and Paul met again for coffee and conversation at their favorite café. This was their first meeting since each of them had discovered Martin Buber's influence. As a result, each felt more confident, more open to speak with the other.

Paul began with a question he had thought of asking Peter but never had the courage to ask. Looking directly into Peter's eyes Paul asked, "I've indicated to you on several occasions things I really admire about you. And yet you have never identified any of my character traits which you really admire. What might one of them be?"

Peter looked up at Paul with a grin and said, without hesitation: "Fidelity to the task. You complete whatever it is you begin."

Now, both Peter and Paul expressed themselves more directly, more intimately than before. Now, neither person was interested in appearing in any way that was different from who they really were. Now, each of them exhibited fidelity to the task.

Sacramental Dialogue

Midway through last winter, in the afternoon mail, I imagined that I received a strange first class postcard. Of all things, my greatest surprise was the postcard, which came not from a friend traveling through Europe. Of all places it was from the Martin Buber Society. Emboldened print filled one side of the card. Reading its tantalizing outline was merely the first step in a much longer, living process, which required dedicated practice to fulfill its purpose. For where authentic dialogue is fulfilled in its being, when practitioners fully turn to one another, express themselves truthfully, and without reserve, there is brought into being an uncanny and fantastic relationship which exists nowhere else. Curious, I held up the post and read it:

> Martin Buber (1878-1965) stands as one of the universal geniuses of the twentieth century. While many studies have attempted to summarize the scope of Buber's philosophical writings, these words highlight key practices of Buber's basic insight—the deeply reciprocal bond existing between genuine interhuman dialogues and supernatural-human relationships. Buber characterized authentic dialogue in whatever sphere as practicing four core elements: turning, addressing, listening, and responding. Every authentic dialogue becomes "sacramental" when it opens out toward transcendence insofar as practitioners address the "superaddressee," glimpse the "Absolute Person," and taste the spirit of elemental togetherness, found nowhere else. The fundamental outcome of engaging in sacramental dialogue, both with others and with Ultimacy, both in public discourse and private meditation is a renewing self-realization of the entire person. As Buber repeatedly described it, we become who we are created to be—dialogical persons—with the responsibility to participate in co-creative, co-revealing, and co-redemptive relationships in that part of the world where we stand.[13]

13. Buber expresses his basic insight as a deep connection between our authentic relation to one another and to the eternal other. See: Martin Buber, *Philosophical Interrogations,* edited by Sidney and Beatrice Rome (New York: Hope, Rinehardt and Winston, 1964), 99. Martin Buber, *The Philosophy of Martin Buber,* 694. Buber uses words such as transcendence, or Ultimacy, or eternal to refer to the Hebraic god. However else God may be—Buber was well aware and appreciative of different values and names used for "God" in various world religions like Allah, Brahman, Tao. Buber's "God" was biblically-based Presence who was, is, and will always be, who is both Wholly other, or *mysterium tremendum,* wholly present, or the absolute Person. For Buber, "God" is a dialogical God who enters into direct, personal relationship with humans through biographical and historical events calling humans to take a stand and make a decision. Buber's working

The phenomenon as described may seem to obfuscate as much as it reveals about renewing our lives until we reread the word "participate" and recall an earlier reading by the physicist David Bohm. In Bohm's book, *On Dialogue*, he introduced the notion of dialogical participation, or what he called "participatory consciousness," in which each person takes part of a shared consciousness. He writes:

> Accordingly, a different kind of consciousness is possible among us, a *participatory consciousness*—as indeed consciousness always is, but one that is frankly acknowledged to be participatory and can go that way freely. Everything can move between us. Each person is participating, is partaking of the whole meaning of the [part-ners] and also taking part in it. We can call that a true dialogue.[14]

The key, it seems to me, is the interrelationship between taking part *of* and taking part *in* a shared consciousness. Herein lies the secret of sacramental dialogue. As the conversation progresses, it becomes clear that the issue is not pimping a commodity, not pushing a product, but rather by taking interhuman responsibility for listening attentively to what the other is saying to you and responding both to what is said and what is asked and what is unsaid but implied. Not only do I accept the postcard's message, I wish I had written it.

When I left the house that morning, I was greeted by thick fog. The air felt almost as if little droplets would begin forming on my face like on a windshield. When I arrived at the University of California, Santa Cruz gym parking lot, I didn't see Skye at first. No stranger to dialogue, we often talked about books or films of mutual interest.

I was thinking about a remark my son-in-law made when he said: "You've got to write something about what you said: 'I write to live and I live to write.'" He was referring to a podcast of an interview in which my daughter asked me questions about my autobiographical book, *A Life of Dialogue*. "It stuck with me, Ken, you should write some more about what you said," he said.

---

assumption is that the eternal cannot be *expressed* (as an intellectual idea in the third person), but only *addressed* (as the invisible other in the second person), who is always present, always ready to be in dialogue with us.

14. Bohm, *On Dialogue*, 30–31.

Just as I departed from my Jeep, I saw Skye walking toward me. The day before, I had mentioned a half hour interview with me that my daughter had posted about my recent book, *A Life of Dialogue*. He then said, "I'm going to listen to it the first chance I get."

"Oh, I get it," Skye said on the following day. "It's conversation as sacrament." He was referring to our conversation, the day before, about the need for face-to-face dialogue. "You get it," I said. "There aren't that many listeners who will dig down to the tap root of this interview as you have. Yes, genuine dialogue is sacramental."

That is, the absolute is released in and through the dialogic conversation. When it is sacramental, it has three voices, not two (mine and yours). There is also a third voice—the voice of the dialogue itself. It speaks in and through our speaking voices, especially when each speaker hears something that they (or the other) says for the first time, or when one voice really addresses a question or issue that other dialogic partners have.

The co-creative third voice casts a transcendent light on our blind spots. It is a voice of interactive intonations that voicelessly challenges literalistic listening and unthinking mimesis, a point of view which cannot be reduced to either person alone, or to a compromise between them. Rather, the third voice is a mutually animated exchange of inspired intelligence.

Taking a Dialogical Stand

Practicing Buber's dialogue brings you to realize the unutterable significance of taking a dialogical stand in life. "Where do *you* stand?" Buber asks. This is the question of questions. Where do *I* stand in life? How do *I* respond?

A most fitting characterization of Buber's teaching and writing is indicated in the Foreword, to his book *Pointing The Way* (1957/1963), which contains a selection of his essays from 1909 to 1954 that he could still stand behind. There, Buber asks readers to bear in mind that he first had to go through the mystical stage, or phase, or stand believing in "a unification of the self with the all-self."[15]

However, he came to realize that being true to the existence in which he found himself, meant deeply engaging those whom he met along the way by taking a relational stand, by deeply listening and responsibly responding to them, by being willing to continue the dialogue in the future.

15. Buber, *Pointing the Way*, xv.

When Buber says, "here is where I stand," he is not referring to a fixed or permanent or inflexible position, but rather to an openness in the present moment, to whatever or whomever he encounters. Here is the heart of the matter—a dialogical stand is and becomes a clearing, an opening for that for which you stand. Standing thus refers to a person's unique intellectual/emotive orientation or bearing from which you go forth to engage the world and from which your dialogue emanates.

According to Buber, everyone is dialogically constructed (both personally and socially) and dialogically directed (both instinctively and verbally). Further, the dialogical partner affirms our reciprocal and reciprocating responsibility in life. My stand, my place in the world, is not just a function of willpower, is not just an attitude of mind. It also embodies an already-existing dimension, the influence of relational grace that joins with my willpower to affect my presence in the world. When I wholeheartedly and unreservedly respond to the other whom I encounter during the flow of events in my life, without holding back, again and again, I am able to become myself.

Standing exactly where you are situated here-and-now points as well, as T. S. Eliot wrote, in the first movement of "Burnt Norton," "to one end, which is always present." This always present, here-and-now presence embodies, for Buber, being fully "here" in this moment without withholding yourself. Notice that this here-and-now presence is not a singular achievement but rather a presence-for-relationship. That is, I am present not for myself, not just to enjoy life more, but to enter into deep contact with you. Why make such a point of this? Because this here-and-now presence prompts us to be present, signals human language, penetrates our souls.

A dialogical stand is a living commitment to practice *turning, addressing, listening,* and *responding* to whomever and whatever we encounter. Here there is neither fixed nor final words; here, there is mutually engaging and being engaged by the other. For this reason, taking a dialogical stand allows for the innermost growth of the self and for the possibility of attaining innate self-realization in a special way specific to each person.

We all have the potential of existing authentically by practicing genuine dialogue. In this culminating image, Buber suggests that the highest human glory—our self-realization—remains true as long as we do not seek to impose it on others, but rather seek to serve others by inducing their own self-realization.

～ ～ ～

Midway through an on-again, off-again rainy March, on a crisp, sun-filled day freshly coloring the vanilla calla lilies, the orange birds of paradise, the crimson begonias, and the polyphones greens, I found myself sitting at my desk appreciating these colors through my picture window, wanting to re-read one of Buber's shortest essays, "Since We [Are] a Dialogue."

At the time, I was pondering a comparison between practicing "genuine dialogue," and "being a dialogue." Was one a version of the other and if so, why does Buber use significantly different names?

On the one hand, genuine (open, mutual, present, honest) dialogue is and continues to be not without some tension between the "dialogians." Each remains convinced of different political, economic, religious, or international points of view, yet each remains fully open to continuing the dialogue.

Remember in Chapter Two, "Addressing," Buber remarks that for genuine dialogue to occur, one needs to accept and affirm the other, even when not agreeing with their convictions, or points of view. Not that viewpoints are off limits. Rather, as Buber indicated, when opposing viewpoints arise in dialogue, while remaining open to theirs, Buber did his best to convince his partner of his own point of view.

In an underappreciated, often overlooked single page commentary on a poem by Hölderlin, "Since We [Are] a Dialogue," Buber takes us a step beyond dialogue, beyond just having a dialogue with another person. Remarkably, he writes:

> We ourselves are the dialogue: we are spoken ... Our being spoken is our existence ... but now Hölderlin promises men that out of their being as dialogue will come a being as song. To the dialogue indeed belongs the persevering in the tension during the nearing; in song all tensions are melted down. Only when those whose dialogue we are sing us are we We.[16]

According to Buber, Hölderlin introduces another type of dialogue, a pure dialogue, a dialogue without tension, a dialogue that becomes a song. According to Buber's commentary, to the extent that each of us reveals our self by fulfilling the speech that we are, from it will come being as song.

Re-consider Buber's powerfully evocative final sentence—"Only when those whose dialogue we are [with whom our being spoken is our existence] sing us are we We." Beyond *having* a dialogue, we *become* a dialogic

16. Buber, *A Believing Humanism*, 85–86.

song, a living genuine We in which, with all the tensions melted down, We become a memorable common song; we become We.

When speaking of Hölderlin's dialogic song, Buber refers to mutually unreserved, undistracted, selfless presence of one's whole being with another's whole being. Such dialogue is tension free, an unbroken living unity of person with person.

With remarkable subtlety, Buber exclaims that when the dialogical relationship is "exemplified in its highest peak . . . the essential difference between the partners persists unweakened, while even in such nearness the independence of [persons] continues to be preserved."[17]

Still, of course, this is rare, plenty rare.

Not so long ago (or is it always happening?), before adding the final stroke to *Martin Buber's Dialogue*, upon finishing eggs scrambled with baby tomatoes, slices of avocado, and chopped grilled chicken, I began sipping my strong Sunday morning coffee. The sun was not shining.

Listening to music by women for everyone on the local university radio station (88.1 FM), I thought it was over. It—this book—was surely finished. The time was here for other-worldly scientists, this-worldly artists and moralists to be critical of, inspired by, and/or to teach and discuss why "dialogue" matters.

"Intellectually thrilling . . . ," I saw a laudable review saying. The review surprised me both with its choice of words, "achieves an end point that sets it apart," and its spot-on attention to what most needs attention today, now, in this instant.

I couldn't walk away, not yet without reciting one more time the transformative value of genuine dialogue—its wholehearted, attentive, deep, responsible engagement—which, like genuine love, is endless. There are no final words. Even you, as you read, are voicing unspoken responses to these idiosyncratic ideas. While dualistically determined opinions, culturally conditioned viewpoints, provocative and evocative disagreements, and breakthrough insights are sprinkled through your/our reading, it is your responsibility to translate my language system into yours. It is as if each reader keeps a notebook while journeying through life—one with a working title, *My Dialogue with Life*.

17. Buber, *Meetings*, 55.

At odd moments, it may come to pass now and then, as circumstances align themselves, a unique title for what you've been writing will spontaneously present itself. In such an innovative fashion, just after the fog lifted, the title of this book articulated itself.

Then I read an interview on the art of comedy, "Jerry Seinfeld Says Jokes Are Not Real Life," in *The New York Times Magazine* (8.19.18, a palindrome which reads the same forwards and backwards). In the interview, Seinfeld is asked:

> **You use Twitter mostly for self-promotion. Why no Twitter jokes?**
>
> I don't hear the laugh. Why waste my time? It's a horrible performing interface. I can't think of a worse one. I always think about people that write books. What a horrible feeling it must be to have poured your soul into a book over a number of years and somebody comes up to you and goes, "I love your book," and they walk away, and you have no idea what worked and what didn't. That to me is hell. That's my definition of hell.[18]

To avoid Seinfeld's imagined hell, I would like to know how you responded to this book—what worked, what didn't? If you would be interested in sharing your comments and feedback like *what* really worked and *what* would you do differently and *how*? Let me know.[19]

The Between (Betweeness)

After years of thinking through, writing, structuring, discussing, editing, dismissing, restructuring, improving, rewriting, reediting, that did it. I had passed the question of having something worth saying. I was now feeling like my way of saying it could work.

I was traveling down a stretch of the road marked Essential Elements. This is, and has been, the story of a journey into unreserved dialogue told through space and time. Now, I had come to the end, almost.

Yet, I had no idea—none—how to write the penultimate paragraph.

I remember reading along the way the story of a professional photographer who said: "If you're not satisfied with your photos, move in closer." But what could that have to do with what I am saying, I wondered.

---

18. Amira, "Jerry Seinfeld Says Jokes Are Not Real Life" *The New York Times Magazine*, 8.19.18.

19. Please, should you like, send your feedback to kramer@cruzio.com.

I had been taking a thinking-through-it walk at my desk. A visitor comes to the back door.

"Hello, Ken, hello!"

"Come in," I said without seeing her.

"Hello Ken. How are you?"

"Ziggy! How are you? You're early. Come in, come in."

"It's good to see you after these long weeks," she said.

As usual, she sat in the swivel chair at the computer desk just to the right side of my desk. I turned my chair to face her full on.

Ziggy, an interreligious practitioner of Zen and Catholicism, came bearing Hanukkah gelt for my grandchildren. And for me, she brought a print of the ancient Pompeii fresco, "Flora with the Cornucopia." We had discussed the significance of this image, which had taken up residence with Ziggy in her recent trip to Italy.

Not only had Ziggy read and studied Buber's work, she also knew that I was working on this book. In fact, she wrote on the back of the print she brought:

> For Ken
>
> always
>
> turning
>
> addressing
>
> listening
>
> responding

Not unlike the back-then younger Flora, I would describe Ziggy as moving through the world dancingly, singingly, poetically. She spreads joy along the way. She's a gatherer, an assembler, an organizer. She excites others to be excited.

"Do you want some coffee or tea?"

"No, thank you. I'm good."

And then eagerly, she asked, "How is your Buber book progressing?"

"Look," I said, "Here's a single page with each of the sub-heads for the first four chapters. I've been using it as an organizational reminder."

Chapter 1: **Turning**

Clear Skies

The Journey

Turn, Turn, Turn

Reflexion (Bending Back on Oneself)

Breaking Through Thinking

Tuning In

Meditation to Mutuality

Pivoting Around

Practicing Turning

Chapter 2: **Addressing**

Back from Italy

Accepting and Affirming

Speaking Ever-New

The Orange-Haired Mortician

"A Great Man," T. S. Eliot Said

"There Are No Great Men," Buber Said

Making (The Other) Present

Addressing Students

Practicing Addressing

Chapter 3: **Listening**

Sun-Filled Voices

"I" Exam

Obedient Listening

Distracted by Distractions

Dialogic Awakening

The Delivery Man

Boldly (Empathically) Swinging

Landauer's Murder: Buber's Silence

Practicing Listening

Chapter 4: **Responding**

The Nurse with a New Hairstyle

A Confirming Dialogue

"What Do You Think?" Buber Asked

Mutual Animated Describing

Peter and Paul

Sacramental Dialogue

Taking a Dialogical Stand

The Between (Betweeness)

Practicing Responding

She sat processing the one-page structure. Suddenly, she said, "Ken, I love your titles, I can't wait to read how you express Buber."

"My dialogue with Buber, you mean"

"Yes. Yes. It helps me so much to understand what he is saying."

"Thank you, Ziggy. I want to ask you a question."

I wanted to talk with her about the impasse that confronted me at this moment. Each time, however, I was about to speak to Ziggy's question, my grandson, Grayson, who has been circling us since eating his chocolate coins that Ziggy brought, wanted to play.

"Grayson," she said, "Come sit on my lap."

As soon as he did, she said, "Now I've got you," wrapping her arms around him. "Now you're in jail." Grayson squealed and squiggled.

The game was on. He knew what she was implying. He struggled to get released, but couldn't get loose.

Laughing and squirming on her lap, and laughing some more, "Here comes an octopus hug. Grayson, do you know how many arms an octopus has?"

But it was too late. His laughing and squirming and laughing were full-throated.

"Eight," she said as she first wrapped one arm around him, then another, and so on until she had given him eight hugs, while all the while resisting every effort he made to break free.

"What other kind of hug do you want?"

"I want a zombie hug, I want a zombie hug," he repeated. By this time, he was ecstatically happy.

"Okay," she said, "Are you ready." And before he could respond to her, Ziggy gave him a zombie squeeze, laughing and squirming and screeching and full of crazy joy, until she pretended to drop him, only to catch him before he hit the ground. Before he hit the ground, his face flashed terror on top of joy on top of anticipation on top of celebration. And again. And again.

More crazy joy: the blend of anxiety and ecstasy, fear and nuts-ness— oh, if only I had a camera.

When Grayson and Ziggy had to leave at the same time, she drew an inclusive circle with her finger around the three of us. Looking deeply into my eyes with her sparkling eyes, she exclaimed: "The Between, the Between."

One of the things I've noticed over the years of practicing living dialogue is that when the other person makes engaging responses, these responses stimulate more engaging responses which, in turn, can generate even more powerfully meaningful responses. Dialogue-generated responses awaken attention.

Do you recall dialogues in which you have lost awareness of time and space? It may be the result of entering the oscillating sphere that Buber calls the "Between," which exists neither solely in you, nor solely in the other, nor solely in the sum of the two, but in an ontological space existing in and around all of us, the space of Being itself in which our Being—who we really are as human beings—awakens.

Around six weeks later, I received a call from Ziggy who was nearby and asked if I had time for a "quick" visit.

"A *visit*, yes," I said. "Quick, I'm not sure." We laughed. Minutes later, she came with a vase of yellow daffodils. "It's almost spring," she said. We hugged. We talked. We listened.

The first thing she smilingly told me was about a recent weekend visit with her daughter in a rented cabin looking out over the Pacific and the deepening levels of conversation they shared. Noticing that her daughter wrote a letter to her husband on the two day trip, as was their practice whenever spending time away from one another, Ziggy wrote a post to her husband.

After Ziggy returned, when her letter arrived the next week, she asked her husband how it made him feel.

"It reminded me of our cross-country courtship forty years ago," he said. Feelings, now forty years later and deeper, emerged again. Rededication occurred.

Into this story, my grandson Grayson runs to hug Ziggy, to ask her if she will play a game with him.

"I'd love to," she said, "but first I want to talk with your grandpa." Just then, the family dog trotted past us toward the kitchen, giving Grayson a new partner to run off with.

"Ziggy," I said, "do you remember the last time you were here?"

"Yes," she said not altogether certain to what I was referring.

"Remember, as you were about to leave; you were standing over there," I said pointing to the sliding glass door, "right there, before you left, you exclaimed, 'it's the *between*, it's the *between*.' What did you mean then by the term 'between'?"

"Oh," Ziggy said somewhat surprised, "I was talking about Grayson, about the unconditional love he reflected between us."

As a look of "aha" spread across my face, she said, "It was Grayson's light—the light of unconditional love that is what I was referring to."

Practicing Responding

Like opening your eyes to see the grandeur of a new day, walking this dialogic path involves opening yourself (through these four specific practices) and genuinely engaging and being engaged by others and in the process rediscovering who you really are.

Practicing responding is the direct expression of our human birthright, a way of engaging and being engaged—authentically—by others and, in the process, rediscovering who we really are. If I say to you, "This practice has altered my life, it would be because, although I didn't always get what I wanted, by practicing responding, I certainly got what I needed." And if you say to me, "Ok, but: how, specifically can I practice responding?"

Perhaps all you have to do is observe what happens when you do not practice responding. To realize *what* you need to do and *how* you, in your unique humanness, can best do it, for the other person as well as for yourself.

Try it; you'll see. Here's how it can be portrayed.

Trusting dialogue

Honestly **Responding** **Honestly**

Trusting dialogue

Responsibly Responding

Honestly to what is said

- Unreservedly: without leaving anything out
- Courageously: willing to be vulnerable in a common situation

Trusting what isn't said

- The co-creative nature of the dialogical process itself
- The sacramental potential of practicing genuine dialogue

Here, it is crucial to understand that in order to respond fully to the other, it is necessary to become aware not only of what the other says through our senses, but what they are thinking and feeling and experiencing at that moment. Responding is not just a part of human nature, a part of social ritual, a part of family rites of passage, but is a very intimate interaction between specific persons who willingly trust the process of dialogue.

PART III
Exemplifications

5

Interview-Dialogue with Kobun Chino Roshi[1]

THE FOLLOWING TWO EXEMPLIFICATIONS, or interview-dialogues are expansive uses of interhuman exchanges. Each of these exchanges focuses on "Death and Dying," and is offered through a dialogical lens in that the interviewer begins with one pre-planned question and then follows the spontaneous spirit of the dialogues. I specially consider different cultural-spiritual identities: Japanese-Zen and American-Hasidic. It features words by Kobun Chino Roshi, Zen teacher of Steve Jobs (iconoclastic, artistic genius who reshaped our domestic lives), among others, and Professor Maurice Friedman, student of Martin Buber turned teacher of Buber.

KRAMER: *I am with Kobun Chino Roshi, a man who defies all labels, a man who was sent to America twenty-five years ago by his Japanese Zen Master, and a man who has, over the years, taught thousands of American Zen students the practice of Zazen (seated Zen). Kobun, you once said: "When I sit, the world sits." Now, I understand that those who know need no explanation, and for those who don't know, no explanation is possible. Still, could you tell us what you meant by that remark?*

KOBUN: The phenomena of how you have been experiencing things (everything according to your understanding of it) depends on the relationship of the external world to your internal perception. What I meant by "I sit: the world sits" is that everything sits.

1. I conducted this interview with Kobun Chino Roshi in a Death, Dying, and Religions class at San Jose State University in 1991. It has not been previously published.

Is it possible that when you sit there is a sense in which you don't sit?

You have come to a point in which something is happening to you. Did it happen before? Sitting does not always mean what your mind thinks it means.

Would you say, then, that in order to really hear what is being said one has to allow their mind to sit, in silence?

That is the mind's natural way.

Kobun, if in this conversation who I am (as someone raised in a completely different tradition from yours) becomes clarified by virtue of our differences, in what way does who you are become clarified by who I am?

Maybe who we are can never be known. Maybe there is nothing that explains who you are, not even the words "man" or "woman."

Well, let me shift the direction a bit to ask: What is your purpose in life?

My constant concern is to go back to who I truly am, to understand where I really am, to understand who I was.

Is who I truly am who we all truly are?

Yes.

How is it possible for you not to be who you are?

To stop breathing. By breathing, you discover that you are here. Without noticing your breath, you are actually everywhere.

When you sit, your breathing shifts, quiets, transforms, so to speak, from your ordinary breathing. When you sit for a long period of time, would it be correct to say that you forget who is breathing?

Not quite. You are aware of it. Sometimes you can't totally forget. Your breathing naturally slows down. Usually, when you sit like this, you start in a conscious way. And then, after a while, you only need half as much breath.

Let me ask a question about death in this context. Is it possible, through sitting as you do, to have at best an analogous experience of death, to enter into the presence of death (in meditation), such that an awareness of death itself opens up which you don't experience in other ways?

On some level, it always opens up, not by intellectual understanding. Where is your past? Where did it go? That is my question. My death is in the past, not in the future. If it was in the future, it would not have come yet. This is an ongoing realization that my death is pure imagination. It has not happened yet.

What do you mean—it "is in the past?" For most people it is in the future.

What I meant is that death, as you know it, happened to your grandparents, let us say. Where have they gone? You might say, they disappeared in you. They are now inside you, and you still don't see them. But your eyes, and your height and your looks show where they are. And yet, they are dead you say. Yes, they are dead.

Yes, I understand. Could it not also be said that one lives into the future by dying to the past, and that, in fact, this is a liberating way to live?

If you are present in the future, even that belongs to the present.

Perhaps we could shift to your experience of being raised in a Buddhist Temple and, in the process, witnessing death and seeing dead bodies.

It is a Buddhist family custom that when someone is passing on a messenger comes to the Temple to ask for a priest to be there. A priest took me many places like that. At the moment a person is about to pass away, the whole family gathers around to say goodbye to this person. Sutra chanting takes place about the time the dying person can't communicate. That is the last teaching of the Sakyamuni Buddha in the *Parinirvaba Sutra*. It's a long Sutra, which takes about forty-five minutes to recite. So the person who passes away soaks or absorbs it into their mind. The Buddha's last teaching is in this Sutra. The family also quietly listens.

Kobun, in many traditions, the last words or the last thoughts of the dying person are said to be very crucial with regard to the passage through death. In the Bhagavad Gita, *for instance, Krishna says that at death one should "Meditate on me!" Is there a similar type of instruction in your tradition which teaches a dying person to meditate on Sakyamuni Buddha, or to repeat certain words to themselves as they are dying?*

It depends on how the person passes away. It is not a moment of passing on. It is, of course, a process that takes several months or a few years. A person begins to prepare earlier. So, one is encouraged to recite the name of the Buddha. We say, "Namo Kya Buddha." "Kya" means "going back." "Namo" is a Sanskrit word; it is like "O" or "Ah"—you are giving up your own self-notions. You say in English, "OK, I'm ready." In the Chinese character, "Kya" means going back to where you came from. Buddhism is about realizing where you came from. You lived as a human Buddha of many kinds. And finally, you say, "So now I am going back to Buddha. That's how the world goes." The actual experience of each person is a state of faith—not knowledge, but faith.

That may surprise a few people, since Western traditions seem to emphasize faith more than Eastern traditions, especially Zen Buddhist traditions. So perhaps you could say a word about what you mean by "faith."

Faith means "no doubt, no doubt about what you are doing or thinking." It means also self-confidence. Not an artificial or put-on kind of confidence.

What is it like to be this way, to be self-confident in the face of death?

I haven't experienced it yet. But with an eight-year-old mind, I observed those people. All of them became holy creatures in my eyes because of how they suffered. In a few seconds, their faces changed, their bodies relaxed, they became very peaceful. I will prepare myself for this.

How so Kobun? Let's say that your bodily sensations told you that you were going to die soon. Would you do anything differently than you are doing now? Would you live your life any differently or practice any differently than you are practicing now in order to get ready for death?

Practically nothing will change, though I should go back home to pick up the mess I made. (Laughter). Sitting is a wonderful preparation for death. In the last moment of Seshin, breath goes and then you pass on.

Is there one thing that you would like to say which would summarize what you have said?

No one thing . . . breathe every breath thoroughly. . . quit breathing!

Thank you Kobun for reminding us of what we need to do and for embodying it. Arigato.

6

Interview-Dialogue with
Professor Maurice Friedman[1]

KRAMER: *You once wrote that human beings are the only creatures who know they will die, and who will make this knowledge the foundation of their life. I'm interested in that statement. I wonder if you could begin by elaborating on it. How does knowledge of death affect us as human beings?*

FRIEDMAN: In multiple ways. Obviously, our sense of mortality, our sense of finitude, our sense of limits—our whole relation to time is measured by that. Naturally, we are all so in tune with the types of time, object spans, historical time, that we have a sense of movement from one to another. I do not mean by it exactly the same as Martin Heidegger's *Sein und Zeit* (*Being and Time*)—to be living towards death. I'm not saying that we think about death every moment, but I'm saying nonetheless, it is true as Abraham Joshua Heschel said we should make our life a work of art. That's the very notion that gives shape to our life, not that we are ever finished. I'm not saying that death puts an ending to things that we're doing, but I think we live in tension with death, or think about it. I think a lot less about it now, at least consciously, than I did when I was seventeen.

Why don't you share a little bit about your early thoughts on death?

My own conscious relationship to death began, as I remember, when I was five years old. I could not sleep because of the sudden realization that I would die. I cried until my elder sister came up and comforted me with a statement that I would not die for a very long time. That this did not remove the problem for me was evident from the preoccupation with death

---

1. I conducted this interview with Professor Maurice Friedman at his dining room table in Solana Beach, California, in 1991. It has not been previously published.

that I had during my teens. Sometimes it expressed itself paradoxically in the idea of suicide, which would free me of the tyranny of my body or, as I thought more likely, hand me over to it.

At Harvard, I often thought of Lucretius, who committed suicide on the basis of reasoning that what would come after death would not be so bad as what we have now. This always seemed to me specious, since I had no way of knowing that the "I" would exist at all after death, to be subjected to any experience, good or bad. When I was in high school, I once said to my girlfriend that my whole goal in life was to live long enough to develop a philosophy that would enable me to accept death. Since I have come to know the tales of the Hasidism, I have often been struck by the resemblance to my statement in the Hasidic tale, "The Meaning." When Rabbi Bunam lay dying, his wife burst into tears. He said, "What are you crying for? My whole life was only that I might learn how to die."

I'm interested in Viktor Frankl especially in this connection because of his comment in Man's Search for Meaning *that it was precisely in and through suffering that he came to discover the human vocation. The human vocation was to discover that while everything else could be taken away from a person, the one thing that couldn't be taken away was one's choice of attitude.*

I like a good deal of what Frankl says because his original title was *From Death Camp to Existentialism,* and I like his recognition that it's not just what happens to you—it's your attitude toward it that is part of the event. And I accept his distinction between various types of suffering and types of meaning, one of which comes in an activity that you can do.

What puzzles me most about Frankl's position is his assertion that it is always possible to find meaning. This gives meaning a universal status that divorces it from the very existential and unique situations which Frankl claims give rise to it. There is no room left for the absurd or what I call, "The dialogue of the absurd." Existential trust and existential grace must go together. Frankl's fond of quoting Nietzsche's saying, "Any how can be formed when there is a why." Primo Levi, in *Survival in Auschwitz,* tells how one day as an inmate in the death camp, he reached out his hand for an icicle outside the window to slake his unbearable thirst. A guard came by just then and knocked the icicle down so Levi could not get it. Why, he cried out. Here there is no why, the guard responded. And I say that it is precisely this confrontation with meaninglessness that one can find in every page of Elie Wiesel and Primo Levi, and that I find missing in Frankl. That's a serious question for me personally.

So, what this brings up for me, Maury, is that death itself poses the question of ultimate meaninglessness which no meaning can overcome or soften and that there is something within every human being which finally just has to say, No! I will resist. I will not accept death. Is there something of that in what you're saying about Frankl?

Yes, although I am pointing to what Jaspers called a "limit" situation, "shipwreck." I was struck when Primo Levi said, no analysis of a neurosis—forget it. There is a primal anguish here of the total original chaos. Elie Wiesel remarks, they take it to be a psychological problem, which for him was a metaphysical question. I think they were confronted to be able to maintain it. No one knows that. It would be pure presumption for me to say that. There's a paragraph I wrote, "Death and Dying and the Absurd," in my book, *The Hidden Human Image*, where I say,

> During my years of immersion in mysticism (when I was in the camps in units for conscientious objectors) in the years of the Second World War, I seemed to have developed the philosophy I sought—the beliefs that consciousness is universal, eternal, that there is no individual self, and that the real self cannot die.
>
> But this belief did not stand the test of time or the encounters that made me feel that I'd gone through a sort of death while still alive. Once I would have fully accepted the words of comfort that Rabbi Nachman gave some of his disciples who came weeping to him, complaining that they had fallen prey to darkness and depression and could not lift up their heads either in teachings or in prayer. "My dear sons," Rabbi Nachman said to them, "Do not be distressed by the seeming death which is come upon you, just as on New Year's Day, life ceases and all the stars descend into a deep sleep and awake with a new power shining. So those who truly desire to come close to God must pass through the state of cessation of spiritual life and the falling for the sake of rising." Now I must rebel with Job and Ivan Karamazov, because nights of weariness and months of emptiness mean the passing away of absurdity of our all-too-mortal life.

But I must say it even here, I also accept, Jay Lifton's distinction between ordinary death and absurd death. That is, I think you cannot live without accepting death, and there is no meaning to life if you don't. It's like what Tillich says, "if you can't accept non-being, you can't have being either." But absurd death—the death of the survivors of the atomic bomb, the death in the death camps—is a different matter. So there is a rebellion any of us can make, like Job, but is greatly intensified in these situations. That's why I have called Elie Wiesel the "Job of Auschwitz," and repeated Buber's question, "Can we say, call to God for his mercy endureth forever in the person of Job in the gas chambers?" And that means that the survivors have carried with them not only "survival guilt" as they call it, but the whole person.

Regarding Martin Buber, I have a question that I've wanted to ask you about him for quite some time. You speak about Buber having originally planned to have a chapter in The Knowledge of Man—a chapter on death. And that he decided against that, because as he said to you, "We do not know death in itself, as we know the concrete realities of our existence." In a simple, one paragraph statement (which you translated), Buber once said:

> We know nothing of death, nothing other than the one fact that we shall die—but what is that, dying? We do not know. So it behooves us to accept that it is the end of everything conceivable by us. To wish to extend our conception beyond death, to wish to anticipate in the soul what death alone can reveal to us in existence, seems to me to be a lack of faith clothed as faith. The genuine faith speaks: I know nothing of death, but I know that God is eternity, and I know this, too, that he is my God. Whether what we call time remains to us beyond our death becomes quite unimportant to us next to this knowing, that we are God's—who is not immortal but eternal. Instead of imagining ourselves living instead of dead, we shall prepare ourselves for a real death which is perhaps the final limit of time but which, if that is the case, is surely the threshold of eternity.[2]

And then you respond, while this is true, what we do not know is the anticipation of death—the imagining of death—one's own, and others', and the attitude one brings to the somber and unavoidable future. I'm captured by the phrases, "the anticipation of death," and "the imagining of death," and I wonder if you could explore that a little bit.

I don't mean by the imagining of death, thinking about the personal rites of suicide, and thinking about people finding the note, and the funeral. I'm sure that's a waste of time. No one knows the exact moment of their

---

2. Buber, *A Believing Humanism*, 231.

death. I like the statement in the Talmud in the *Sayings of the Fathers* that you should act as if each day is the day before your death. And that's what I mean by the anticipation of death. The awareness of death is on the horizon. And that seems to give the nod to Heidegger perhaps as against Sartre. Sartre says that death is the "swallowing of the self." This is undoubtedly true, but our anticipation is taken into our subjectivity and is an important part of it. And Buber is fully aware of that. For example, he talks about that fear of abandonment, which is a foretaste of death.

In my reflections on existential guilt, I'm looking at a passage from Buber's "Guilt and Guilt Feelings," which enables us to do what he suggests has to be done. Existential guilt is guilt where we take ourselves as burdens in a personal situation, and guilt that comes out of injuring another. Buber says we have to illuminate that, I who am so different am nevertheless the person who did that, and persevere in that illumination. The next step is repairing: existence through acts of "remorse."

One of the things I've treasured about Viktor Frankl is his recognition that "potentialism" is just the beginning, but never the ending. We have to put aside the other nine hundred and ninety-nine possibilities out of a thousand and choose this one and live with it. And I thought that critique of the potentialist movement was very sound. So at the same time, when Buber calls Heidegger's philosophy a "nightmare," and I suspect he does so from the standpoint of Heidegger's focus on *Sein und Zeit*, I think that it's because Buber would say there's a bridge over the abyss of the universe. And I think that abyss is the abyss of death. In other words, the end is an affirmation—that love is stronger than death, and no way does it underplay death though, and that's very important. But, it's one thing to say the anticipation or awareness of death is mixed with every moment and it will affect the whole sense of self. It's quite a different thing to say, as Heidegger does, that it individualizes me down to my *dasein* in such a way that ontologically it is non-relational. So while he would say that *dasein* is *mit sein*—to be there is to be there with the other—on the ontic level. Ontologically, he is very clear about this.

Let me extend the question to the anticipation of after death. So human beings are almost inevitably thrown into this question of wonderment: What happens to individual, personal consciousness—the "I,"—after death? Now from your perspective, how would you respond to that?

Martin Marty wrote a full-page review of my third volume on Buber's life, the later years, in the *New York Times* and he quotes Catherine Whiteside Taylor, the remarkable Jungian therapist who had gotten to know Buber in his later years. She asked Buber, "Have you ever thought about the question of life after death?" And Buber said, "Who has not?" But to imagine ourselves in a life after life is to make death unreal, to rob it of some of its reality. I feel that it's a very Jewish attitude. The book of Job says, a tree cut down can grow again, but a human cannot. The sons may come to grief, but you will not know it. And while it's perfectly true, perhaps through Zoroastrian sources, about the time of the Pharisees, a different notion came into Judaism. Even the Pharisees said, "a day in the world to come is better than this—an hour of mitzvoth in this life is better than a thousand years in the world to come." They did not remove attention from the present to the future.

Since I know that you have written about your various dialogues with religious traditions, with different thinkers, philosophers, human beings, and in fact, your life is a life of dialogue, I'm curious to know if you have a discrete, unique dialogue with death itself.

I think I had one perhaps, when I was young. I thought when I was seventeen that I would die at twenty two. I don't know why, well I do and I do not. I don't think about it that much. On the other hand, for example, I think it enters my dreams more than my conscious thought, and from time to time I come up against a dream. I also shared with my wife—she's almost my age, not quite—a various curious sense, it's not all the same as I might be killed in a war or in an accident. But simply excluding all those ever-present possibilities that I've always talked about, Melville saying in *Moby Dick*, "if you were a philosopher you would feel no more secure at home with a poker in your hand by the fire than if you went out in an open boat at sea with harpoon lines whizzing about you." But now there was something else. Now there is the awareness of the sharp sense. I am now seventy two. My father died at age seventy seven, I don't have to live as long as he did or die as soon as he did, but it's in my consciousness, and not just that, but this very clear sense that well, five years, seven years, down the line. It's a rather strange thing. It does do something. I don't think that it necessarily makes me feel lonely or anything like that, but it does in some way change my relation to things. Like there is blank space isn't a very good way to put it, but there's like an extra dimension—an extra mid dimension that is an unfilled dimension rather than a filled one.

How does death show up for you in dreams? Do you experience yourself dying in dreams?

No. Not like that. Like a thought that takes place in the dream. Not that I think about dying or something like that—but a clear sense of limitation— that is the end. I think it must happen repeatedly, but not all the time.

Then how do you bring that back into your waking?

I don't bring my dreams back into my waking. Insofar as my dreams stay with me, I have the effect. Then I embody their force. Because I would agree, we don't really have dreams. We never have it exactly the way it was. But it remains as something that speaks to me, and I respond to it in my waking life. I used to write my dreams down. I don't do that anymore. I do try to remember them and often I do and often I don't.

There is a question I have asked many people, and I want to ask you now: What's missing from the way in which most people view or entertain or conceive the idea of death? What's missing from the way most people approach death, the presence of which would better enable them to come to terms with it?

I think I would feel presumptuous in answering that question. I don't want to make judgments of most people. It's the most private part of a person's life, but I'll tell you what came to mind just now. I wrote a book, *The Con-firmation of Otherness*. I have a chapter in it on aging, here I mention Erik Erikson's notion of life's stages we go through. The last one he calls Integrity or Despair. Then I ask a question. I knew Erikson, even in his eighties, was still actively writing and lecturing and so on. He did not commit suicide like Bruno Bettelheim, but he did die a couple of weeks ago. And I was asking a question about him, "Would he have integrity and not despair if he ceased to have generativity?" To remain generative was one of his earlier things. And I knew that was a question I was asking about myself.

We tend most of the time to think of death as an objective event that we can understand through our categories. But when we truly walk in the valley of shadows, the accounts of death tell us something we've really known all along. That life is the only reality that is given to us. That this reality, and not some continuing entity or identity of a personal nature is all that we actu-ally know. We do not know life without our individual selves, but neither do we know ourselves without life. We know death to be sure. Life is reality we share while we are alive. To say that we did not exist and again shall not exist is to make our existence of self nothing. When you are dead and your body is cremated, and the ashes scattered, where are you? This is a question that cannot be answered in objective terms. For it is I myself who asks it of myself and I am impelled to respond. A man must give himself to death but when he has done so, he discovers that he is not to die, but to live.

Thank you Maury for this enlivening and revealing dialogue. I recall, as you once said in a class at San Jose State University, it's a listening, and I would add, a responding process.

Conclusion

"Because the conclusion can't be written," Charlie Mcdowell, the lanky University of California, Santa Cruz professor of computer science replied, looking directly into my eyes. He was serious.

During the fall and winter quarters, when our paths often crossed in the men's pool locker room, we would discuss the art of teaching. He knew I was writing this book and in that context, each time we met, I would teasingly ask him, "Have you started your book yet?"

"No, and I don't think I will." He remarked as he prepared to leave the locker room for his extra-large lecture hall class of more than two hundred students.

"Why not?" I asked, "You could turn the structure of your class into an outline for your book. There it is. Why not?"

His response was completely unexpected. "Because," he said, smiling as he picked up his bag and started toward the door, "like anyone writing a book on computer science knows, before beginning the subject would have already changed dramatically. It's not possible," he remarked, "to keep up with the field, let alone suggest a conclusion about where it might be headed."

He then strode off to his class. If there ever has been a time I wished I knew what another person knew, it was then. Even though I completely accepted the validity of his reason, it did not seem like a road block to me.

As long as there is an intelligent listener to one who speaks (the professor), that listener (in this case, myself) can and will voice a viewpoint that carries the dialogue further.

Recognizing the significant differences between our fields (STEM vs. Humanities), one could still briefly summarize the material that the book has covered, I thought, which would then provide a launching platform into potential futures.

For instance, *Martin Buber's Dialogue: Discovering Who We Really Are* seeks to achieve its goal—*mutuality in speech*—by focusing attention on four elemental practices of genuine dialogue (*turning, addressing, listening, responding*). As Buber indicates, authentic dialogue occurs when: 1) I stand with you in a living partnership, a common situation; 2) I share myself, my basic attitude with you; and 3) I listen attentively and respond responsibly to you without withholding anything.

Thinking about what the University of California, Santa Cruz professor had said a few days later, and then again a few days after that, I was left pondering the question: What would Buber himself say? Would it even be possible for him (for anyone?) to look back on their entire life to discern its conclusive key insight?

Others, who have studied Buber's writings with great appreciations, have asked him in his mid-seventies: "What is the chief conclusion expressible in conceptual language of [your] experiences and observations?" Buber decisively responded: "I can give no other reply than confess to the knowledge comprehending the questioner and myself: to be [human] means to be the being that is over-against. The insight into this simple fact has grown in the course of my life."[1]

Buber's key insight leads to just this: what matters most for humans is taking a stand over against the other—being-with-others, person with person, interrelatedness, becoming aware of the other's self. As a result, ever and again a common presence simultaneously enables understanding and confirming the other. Each person becomes both authentically human and uniquely self-realized.

Here we portray the four core elements of "genuine dialogue," which Buber presented and whose liberating interactions become clearer the more we practice them.

1. Buber, *Meetings*, 57.

Genuine Dialogue's Core Elements

1. **Turning Wholeheartedly**

   Away from self

   - Away from self-affirming interests, narratives, assumptions, and thoughts
   - Away from distractions, appearances, and impositions

   Toward the other

   - By "temporarily suspending" one's own attitudes and beliefs
   - By openly surrendering into relationships with the other (person, nature, animal, art, music . . .)

2. **Addressing Attentively**

   Accepting the other

   - No matter their political, religious, ethical, cultural beliefs, just like you
   - The other's presence regardless of race, culture, gender, sexual preference

   Affirming the other

   - As a unique person who has the same right to speak and be heard as you do
   - The other's right to express beliefs and viewpoints even when different from yours

3. **Listening Deeply**

   To what is said

   - Openly and receptively even when the other disagrees with your viewpoints
   - Without analyzing, associating, or judging the other person

   To what isn't said

   - What is inferred beneath the spoken or unspoken words
   - By boldly swinging to the other's side to imaginatively feel, think, experience what the other is feeling, thinking, experiencing

4. **Responding Responsibly**

Honestly to what is said

- Unreservedly, without leaving anything out
- Courageously, willing to be vulnerable in a common situation

Trusting what isn't said

- The co-creative nature of the dialogical process itself
- The sacramental potential of practicing genuine dialogue

Beyond Dialogue

But what is beyond unreserved dialogue? What is open, truthful, fully present, and mutual? What's beyond fully turning and addressing, listening and responding to one another? What would happen if persons (both individually and culturally) recognized the inestimable value of authentic dialogue for a worthwhile life, not to mention human survival?

In the midst of pondering possibilities that came to mind, my daughter Leila entered my office and sat at the computer table next to my desk. Then, as often happens to me (to you, too, I'm sure), in the midst of thinking about how to conclude this work, she asked, "Dad, what would a world without dialogue be like?" It was a question that immediately struck me deeply.

"My entire book," I said, "addresses how to avoid stumbling into that strange world. It would be a world of last words, words spoken with authoritative, monological attitudes as if the speaker was always right, words that silence others. This book is about the opposite: how living words bring people alive. The beauty of genuine dialogue—where you are fully present to the other's presence, turning to them with the intention of establishing a living mutual relationship. If one of the partners speaks a last word, dialogue ends. Unthought-of possibilities end. Co-creativity ends. Deep listening ends."

Philosopher of language Mikhail Bakhtin suggests, in a dialogic field there is no final word (nor should there be). Neither I, nor you, nor any of us should want to speak the final word about anything! There is always a new idea, a fresh possibility.

The next dialogical adventure, the never-thought-of insight arises in our traveling this path together. We question answers, share our wonders and wonderings, and help each other deal with issues, situations, circumstances.

Traveling together on this path, as we have been, rescues each of us from our solo journeys that trap us in the seemingly deft nature of our own expertise. Sharing the same path, breathing in the same air and space and light along the way, we walk again and again helping each other through broken dreams and joyless days. We re-discover ourselves, in walking, talking, listening, and responding. We have no way of knowing what is waiting for us, yet we know where we stand. How invigorating!

When David Bohm came to the end of his brilliant work, *On Dialogue*, he responded to the question, "What's beyond dialogue" in this way:

> "The question is really: do you see the necessity of this process? That's the key question. If you see that, it is absolutely necessary, then you have to do something."[2]

> "And, as a result," he continues,

> "It could make a new change in the individual, a change in the relation to the cosmic. Such an energy has been called 'communion' . . . From a Greek word, *koinonia*, the root of which means 'to participate'—the idea of partaking of the whole and taking part in, not merely the whole group, but the whole."[3]

It took me years and then years more to discover how to practice being dialogical, and to discern the transforming effect it can have in one's total life. Like one's first sip of freshly brewed organic coffee in the morning, becoming dialogical enlivens the entire situation in which we find ourselves.

This is why *turning, addressing, listening,* and *responding* to the other has now become the only possible, plausible, and prolific tool for my life's travels. I say tool as one could say the piano is a tool for enabling magnificent music. Just as striking ivory and ebony keys ignite sounds and singing voices, so does speaking and listening; listening and responding ignites us to become co-creative partners.

To the extent that each of us reveals ourselves to the other in mutual speech—our human birthright—the Universe speaks in and through us. It is as We, ever again as We that our common speaking has meaning and significance. When our dialogic voices resound together, We discover that We exist, in the realest sense, in the dialogue itself.

I hear Maurice Friedman say, as he once did in class, "Five years after I published *Martin Buber: A Life of Dialogue*, I wrote to Buber saying that

2. Bohm, *On Dialogue*, 54.
3. Ibid.

if I were to write the book again, I would add a conclusion titled '*Existential Trust.*'" It seems to me that 'Existential Trust' is "the real heart of your teaching."

Buber replied "You are right. Existential trust is indeed the heart of the attitude underlying my life and thought."[4] It is this existential trust—a willingness to go forth and meet the unique present rather than take refuge in what is already known—that Friedman wanted to highlight.

Trust: trust in existence, in openness to the other and in mutual transformation that happens between persons in real dialogue. Trust: accepting the unpredictably unique challenge that each new moment brings. Trust: in existence as it presents itself to us in each new moment. Trust embodies the courage to be responsible in each new situation. The final two sentences in Friedman's *Touchstones of Reality* book read:

> The smog of existential mistrust through which we move need not prevent our making ever-new contact with reality. If we dare to trust, we can grow in the courage to address and the courage to respond.[5]

A Time to Speak

One of the invigorating qualities of dialogue is, as we have mentioned, "there is no last word." And so it is with this book. Each time I think I'm finished with an idea, with a section, with an association, something else shows up to be added.

Just as there is no last word, there is as well always a time to speak. Realizing the utter impossibility of ending these words, I received an email from a dear friend, Harold Kasimow (Professor Emeritus at Grinnell College). He sent me an attachment that he was sending to Huffington Post in which he addressed the Charlottesville, VA, incident (August 12, 2017).

Harold begins his comments with two quotations. The first: "Silence in the face of evil is itself evil . . . Not to speak is to speak. Not to act is to act;" the second: "Darkness can't drive out darkness; only light can do that. Hate can't drive out hate; only love can do that." One quotation is from a Lutheran pastor Dietrich Bonhoeffer who died in Nazi Germany; the other is from a Baptist minister Martin Luther King Jr. who, like Bonhoeffer, was assassinated because of his stand against bigotry and hatred.

---

4. Heard in a graduate seminar at Temple University, 1968.
5. Friedman, *Touchstones of Reality*, 331.

In this time of bigotry and hate speech, anti-Semitism and Islamophobia, Harold writes, "We must respond in a way that makes a difference." Yes, I agree, and I think readers of this book certainly have necessary tools available to them.

Answering his own question "What can we do?," Harold points to the story of an African American musician Daryl Davis. Harold comments that for many years Davis has been practicing dialogue by making friends with members of hate groups. By listening to, and speaking with them, he has influenced some of them to leave their groups.

Redirecting Harold's own words originally addressed to Davis himself, with Harold's permission, I readdress them to him: "I am in awe of his ability to see that we are all interrelated, and bring about a revolution of the heart in some of the people we meet."[6]

But finally, this book is an homage to Martin Buber, about whom my teacher, Maurice Friedman, rightfully and respectfully called, "one of the universal geniuses of our time." Yes, I say, Yes. Not only has Buber retrieved the inestimable value and transformative power of "genuine dialogue," he has also demonstrated the necessity of practicing it, no, of living it.

I can think of no better way to conclude than by sharing with you one of my favorite passages from Buber's *The Knowledge of Man*. Together, these words have continued to both plumb the earth's depths and simultaneously sing of stars and planets in the heavens. What happens to you as you encounter and are encountered by these words Buber brings into being:

> But where the dialogue is fulfilled in its being, between partners who have turned to one another in truth, who express themselves without reserve and are free of the desire for semblance, there is brought into being a memorable common fruitfulness which is to be found nowhere else. At such times, at each such time, the word arises in a substantial way between [humans] who have been seized in their depths and opened out by the dynamic of an elemental togetherness. The interhuman opens out what otherwise remains unopened.[7]

6. These excerpts were taken from an email Professor Kasimow sent me in which he informed me that his op-ed piece was finally published in the *Des Moines Register* on Sept. 22, 2017. They changed my title to "How Can We Fight Hatred with Love."

7. Buber, *The Knowledge of Man*, 86.

Works Cited

Alda, Alan. *If I Understood You, Would I Have This Look on My Face?* New York: Random House, 2017.

Bohm, David. *On Dialogue.* New York: Routledge Classics, 2006.

Buber, Martin. *Between Man and Man.* Translated by Ronald Gregor Smith and Maurice Friedman. New York: Mcmillan, 1965.

———. *A Believing Humanism.* Translated by Maurice Friedman. New York: Simon & Schuster, 1965.

———. *I and Thou.* Translated by Ronald Gregor Smith. New York: Scribner, 1958.

———. *The Knowledge of Man: Selected Essays.* Edited by Maurice Friedman. Translated by Maurice Friedman and Ronald Gregor Smith. New York: Harper & Row 1965.

———. *The Letters of Martin Buber.* Edited by Nahum N. Glatzer. New York: Schocken, 1991.

———. *Meetings.* Translated by Maurice Friedman. LaSalle, IL: Open Court, 1973.

———. in Paul Arthur Schilpp edition of, *The Philosophy of Martin Buber.* LaSalle, IL: Open Court, 1967.

———. *Pointing the Way.* New York: Harper & Row, 1963.

Friedman, Maurice, *Encounter on the Narrow Ridge.* New York: Paragon, 1991.

———. *My Friendship with Martin Buber.* New York: Syracuse University Press, 2013.

———. *Martin Buber and the Eternal.* New York: Human Sciences, 1986.

———. *Martin Buber's Life and Work.* Vol. 1. New York: Dutton, 1981.

———. *Martin Buber: The Life of Dialogue.* Chicago: University of Chicago Press, 1955.

———. *Touchstones of Reality: Existential Trust and the Community of Peace.* Toronto: Clarke, Irwin, 1972.

Hodes, Aubrey. *Martin Buber: An Intimate Portrait.* New York: Viking, 1971.

Isaacs, William. *Dialogue and the Art of Thinking Together.* New York: Random House, 1999.

Mendes-Flohr, Paul, ed. *Martin Buber: A Contemporary Perspective.* The Library of Jewish Philosophy. New York: Syracuse University Press, 1984.

Nishitani, Keiji. *Nishida Kitaro.* Berkeley: University of California Press, 1991.

Steindl-Rast, Brother David. *I Am Because of You.* New York: Paulist, 2017.

Index

Made in the USA
Columbia, SC
02 January 2021

30172386R00105